THE DEVELOPMENT OF
ENGLISH THEOLOGY IN THE
LATER NINETEENTH CENTURY

THE DEVELOPMENT OF
ENGLISH THEOLOGY IN THE
LATER NINETEENTH CENTURY

Being the Burroughs Memorial Lectures
for 1950
Delivered in the University of Leeds

by

L. E. ELLIOTT-BINNS, D.D., F.R.Hist.S.

ARCHON BOOKS
1971

FIRST PUBLISHED 1952
REPRINTED 1971 WITH PERMISSION OF
LONGMANS, GREEN AND CO. LTD.
IN AN UNALTERED AND UNABRIDGED
EDITION

LIBRARY OF CONGRESS CATALOG CARD NUMBER: 72-122411
INTERNATIONAL STANDARD BOOK NUMBER: 0-208-01045-9

Printed in the United States of America

PREFACE

THE object of the course of lectures here printed was to continue the study begun by Canon Storr in his well-known volume *The Development of English Theology in the Nineteenth Century*. That volume ended at 1860, and it had been Canon Storr's intention, unhappily never fulfilled, to bring his inquiry down to the close of the century. Canon Storr's work was on a comparatively massive scale. To continue it on similar lines within the compass of six lectures was out of the question. Much therefore had to be presented in a summarized form, omitting details and even some of the evidence which lay behind the views set forth. Such a method of treatment was necessary, since a wide field had to be covered, for theology cannot be isolated, and the study of its development in any particular era demands also the consideration of the many currents of thought, and even of action, which were then prevalent. Some of these currents were new; but most of them flowed from the earlier years of the century, attaining fresh force and significance. All alike affected, in a greater or lesser degree, both the contents of theology and the particular form in which it found expression.

We are too near to the nineteenth century for any final attempt to assess the real value of its contribution to theology, but quite clearly it represented a definite and extremely important stage of development. At the same time we must be on our guard against reading back into it advances which have occurred since, for it is only too easy to view what was then promulgated in the light of our own later knowledge.

As the lectures were delivered to an audience many of whom were neither theologians, historians, nor philosophers, the endeavour was made to present the matter in as simple a form as possible, and especially to avoid the use of too many technical terms. Moreover, although the development of theology was the subject of the course, much attention was paid to religion, and to the notions prevalent, not only among thinkers, but also among the general public; for these are more important than is often supposed. The whole history of the Church shows how popular demands may influence Christian practice, and eventually Christian theology. In any case theology and religion can only be separated to their common deprivation; for while religion supplies theology with many of its raw materials, theology, in turn, has the task of arranging religious ideas and practices in order and of purifying them from unworthy elements. In so far as it is successful it deepens them and adds to their effectiveness.

The lectures are printed in the form in which they were delivered, save for a few verbal alterations. A few footnotes have been added by way of illustration or in support of statements made in the text.

L. E. E - B.

SYNOPSIS

Lecture One

THE POSITION IN 1860

AT the outset of this course of lectures, which is in a sense a continuation of Canon Storr's *Development of English Theology in the Nineteenth Century*, I should like to make it clear that the choice of subject was not my own, and that it was only after much hesitation that I consented to accept my present office. To treat the subject at all adequately in six lectures is an impossible task. I am also conscious of serious gaps in my equipment to do so. Canon Storr was pre-eminently a philosopher. Such I cannot claim to be, for though I have done considerable work on medieval philosophy, my knowledge of more modern systems has been chiefly obtained from text-books.[1]

But if I am conscious of my own inadequacy to deal with the subject I am most profoundly convinced of its importance. What is needed to-day above all things is theological leadership and a presentation of the Christian belief and way of life which men can understand and appreciate. They feel that much in Christianity, as popularly conceived, has been rendered obsolete by the advance of knowledge, and, unassisted, are unable to distinguish between its permanent elements and the transient forms in which they are embodied.

Theologians, like other thinkers, are tempted to live in a private world of their own. To do so certainly

[1] For an admirable treatment of the philosophical side see C. C. J. Webb, *Religious Thought in England from 1850*.

B   I

simplifies their problems. They, and religious leaders with them, are naturally conservative and not at all anxious to make concessions to demands for restatement. But if religion is to survive as a living and effective force, sooner or later such concessions must be made. A study of conditions in the later nineteenth century and of the influences which induced theologians, slowly indeed and often grudgingly, to make concessions is surely of immense value. For the problems which they faced are still with us, though our method of treatment may have altered its emphasis; for them the primary line of approach was historical and metaphysical, whereas now it has become more psychological, and even liturgical. At the same time a knowledge of the rapidly changing conditions of that century and a comparison with those of to-day will reveal the danger, and this is an excuse for much theological caution, of attempting a premature synthesis. 'If you marry the Spirit of your generation,' Dean Inge once said, 'you will be a widow in the next.'[1]

In our study we shall be treading well-worn ground, but it merits fresh examination; for every passing year enables us to see things in truer perspective, even if the time has not yet come to pass a final judgement on the achievements of English theology in the later nineteenth century.

Before commencing a detailed examination of our period I must refer to some important factors in the situation of which lack of space forbids fuller treatment. I mean the numerous social, economic, and political developments which then took place. If their effect was indirect it was often considerable; for life and thought inevitably react upon one another, and in facing the novel challenges which those changing conditions made urgent, theologians and religious leaders came to a fresh realiza-

---

[1] *Diary of a Dean*, p. 12.

tion of the scope and potentialities of the Gospel message. In a tentative way a new idea of Christian Ethics was being worked out, as well as an approach to a more developed moral theology. It can be seen in the writings of men like Maurice, Westcott, and the *Lux Mundi* group among others.

Two events seem to me to have had special importance —the repeal of the paper duty in 1860, and the beginnings of a national system of education—though their full effects were not immediately evident, not even by the end of our period.

The repeal of the paper duty and the enormous increase in the number of those who could read gave to the press an influence which it had never before enjoyed. This meant, among other things, that ideas, and not least religious ideas, circulated more freely, and over a much wider area. There was in consequence a growth of popular interest in theological questions and, as a further consequence, an insistent demand on the part of the more thoughtful laity for guidance, and even for a modification of the traditional theology. To us the extent to which theological subjects found a place in the press is surprising. Aubrey Moore wrote in the 'eighties: 'No periodical is complete without an article in which Christianity is defended or attacked.'[1] Predominant among such periodicals was *The Fortnightly Review* which for many educated people, especially among the growing generation, had almost the authority of a 'gospel,' and in nearly every number there was some attack on orthodoxy. This was part of a definite policy as John Morley made clear: 'Literature was a weapon, an arm, not merely a literary art.'[2]

Popular interest in theology is reflected in the oft-

[1] *Science and the Faith*, p. 113.
[2] *Recollections* I, p. 100.

quoted lines from Browning's *Gold Hair*, published in 1864:

> The candid incline to surmise of late
>   That the Christian faith proves false, I find:
> For our Essays and Reviews debate
>   Begins to tell on the public mind,
> And Colenso's words have weight.

This quotation from Browning brings out another remarkable thing in connexion with the growing interest in theology—the displacement in the popular mind of the official guardians and exponents of the faith by literary guides. This was, of course, not entirely novel; Milton, for example, had exercised a profound influence on the religious ideas of the multitude; but there was one striking difference, it was now being exercised on a much wider scale, and not merely upon the multitude. In the opinion of Hastings Rashdall, 'Tennyson and Browning were the greatest theological teachers of their generation';[1] whilst Robertson Smith affirmed that the impression made upon him by *Ecce Homo* was nothing like so deep as that made by *Christmas Eve* and *Easter Day*.[2] For the secret of all this I think we may turn to the introduction to T. H. Green's *Prolegomena to Ethics*, published in 1868, where he says that in poems such as *In Memoriam* and *Rabbi Ben Ezra* 'many thoughtful men find the expression of their deepest convictions.' That is why they turned away from the professed theologians, with their attitude of reserve and restraint, to guides who were as free as themselves. Perhaps after all the real essence of Christianity can best be expressed in terms of poetry rather than of dogmatic theology. This, however, does not mean that I agree with Santayana when from his monastery in

---

[1] Matheson, *Life of Hastings Rashdall*, p. 177.
[2] Black and Chrystal, *William Robertson Smith*, p. 535.

Rome he recently wrote: 'As in poetry, so in religion, the question whether the events described actually occurred is trivial and irrelevant."[1]

One at least, however, who was a true poet, chose another way; and when his mind became obsessed with theological speculations he abandoned poetry for prose. I refer, of course, to Matthew Arnold. For him the essential function of literature was the reconstruction of the foundations of theology, and he certainly made some contribution to that end, for Professor Percy Gardner considered that *St. Paul and Protestantism*, which appeared in 1870, contained 'the best account of the Pauline theology' that he knew.[2] But on the whole Matthew Arnold exercised a subversive rather than a constructive influence. Many of his ideas were made popular by the novels of his niece, Mrs. Humphry Ward, especially by *Robert Elsmere*, published in 1888. Another woman novelist who exercised great influence and helped to spread views critical of orthodoxy was George Eliot.

So much for preliminary remarks. We come now to deal with the situation as it existed at the beginning of our period. Some of the influences then at work had already been operative in the early part of the century, but were now becoming more powerful and manifest; they had gained sufficient force to overcome the barriers which had been erected against them. Soon, new tides of influence would mingle with them until they became an overwhelming flood.

Many of these influences were personal, for the Victorian Age was an age of prophets, and took much of its tone from great names rather than from systems of thought. In a sermon to Cambridge undergraduates in February 1909 Bishop Percival described life at Oxford

[1] *The Idea of Christ in the Gospels*, p. 10.
[2] *The Religious Experience of St. Paul*, p. vii.

fifty years before. 'Its thought was inspired and dominated by unusually great personalities, Carlyle, Ruskin,
Wordsworth, Shelley, Tennyson, Bentham, Mill; these
were the names to conjure with. Browning, Spencer,
Darwin were just rising above the horizon.'[1] Carlyle was
certainly hailed as a prophet, denouncing what he regarded as shams, and the young especially were en-
thralled by him and their talk was apt to be full of his
phrases. At the same time he witnessed to the spiritual
nature of reality in an age of growing materialism.
Another 'prophet,' not mentioned by the bishop, was
Emerson. His influence tended to unsettlement, for
though he was an inspiring and stimulating force—John
Clifford, the great Baptist leader, was much influenced by
him[2]—his teaching lacked consistency and had no firm
underlying basis. Coleridge, too, had still an appeal,
though to the more select minds; Hort was greatly
affected by him. He stood for freedom of thought as
against any religion based solely on authority. The real
guide was the spirit of God working in the Church and
in the soul of man.

In studying the effect of the changes in the situation
upon theology may I again remind you that much of it
was indirect, a new atmosphere was being created in
which theology had to learn to live. It is the position as a
whole, not its mere details, that really matters; 'what is
important for us to know of any age,' Morley has said,
'is not its peculiar opinions, but the complex elements of
that moral feeling and character in which, as in their
congenial soil, opinions grow.'[3]

The period was characterized by a vast increase of
knowledge, as also by the influx of new ideas and mental

---

[1] W. Temple, *Life of Bishop Percival*, p. 6.
[2] Marchant, *John Clifford*, p. 12.
[3] *Recollections*, I, p. 72.

activities. Knowledge, indeed, had increased so enormously, and over such wide and varied fields, that it was no longer possible for anyone to master it. Specialization was the order of the day and research had perforce to be broken up into a number of isolated provinces. This not only made the task of the theologian more arduous but it also led to a divorce between the Faith and many forms of human activity and thought; 'as a necessary consequence there was on all sides a want of solidity and comprehensiveness in the religious contribution and a dangerous readiness to accept unverified formulas.'[1]

The Victorians are usually regarded as possessing a spirit of confidence and certitude; but this did not extend to religion and philosophy, especially in the period with which we are concerned. It was no age of faith—and after all a so-called age of faith is generally nothing more than an age of non-inquiry—but supremely an age of doubt and conflict, and also of much inconsistency. For men sought to retain their inherited or instinctive beliefs and at the same time to accept the conclusions of natural science. Moreover, they failed to realize that these conclusions, as they were generally interpreted, were at odds, not only with the traditional forms of belief, but also with the popular notions of freedom and progress. This was the inevitable conclusion, and for its expression we turn again to a poet. Here is the opinion of James Thomson, the author of *The City of Dreadful Night*:

> I find no hint throughout the Universe
> Of good or ill, of blessing or of curse;
> I find alone Necessity Supreme;
> With infinite Mystery, abysmal, dark,
> Unlighted even by the faintest spark.
> For us, the flitting shadows of a dream.

Religious faith, however, was still looked upon as a

[1] Westcott in *Life of E. W. Benson*, II, p. 691.

matter of grave importance. As this is a factor that we may overlook, I must say a little more about it. Religion was, indeed, regarded as so fundamental that without agreement upon it there could be no true friendship or full sympathy and confidence. A pathetic illustration of this may be found in the correspondence between R. L. Nettleship and Henry Scott Holland published in Stephen Paget's life of the latter. In the preface he wrote: 'I hope I have not done wrong to make a free use of R. L. Nettleship's letters, they belong to a time when differences of belief were taken gravely, as a tragedy, which now are taken lightly, as a comedy.'[1]

This concern over religion had another effect besides the severing of friendships, for it led many who were critical of orthodox Christianity still to maintain an outward conformity. Among them were J. A. Froude, the historian, a former disciple of Newman, and Matthew Arnold, who, when he gave up orthodoxy as a fond but beautiful dream, still clung to the Church, and even tried to bring it to his way of thinking.

The biographies of the later nineteenth century contain not a few records of prolonged, and often indecisive, conflict in the minds of those who sought to reconcile their spiritual needs with their intellectual principles. Examples may be found in the lives of Henry Sidgwick, the philosopher, and John Addington Symonds, the poet and historian. Both were deeply convinced of the need for religion as meeting human longings and also as a basis for morality; yet neither, in spite of continual searching, could ever attain to a settled belief. We may trust that

> from these ploughed-up souls the spirit brings
> Harvest at last,

but the problem of the devoted yet disappointed searcher

[1] *Op. cit.*, p. v.

after truth raises real difficulties, as it had done in past ages, for Aquinas himself had endeavoured to meet it. 'Nor is it the fault of the Word that all men do not attain to the knowledge of the truth, but some remain in darkness. It is the fault of men who do not turn to the Word and so cannot fully receive Him.'[1]

Others, baffled by the flood of new knowledge and finding it impossible to reconcile it with the older faith, frankly gave up the task and plunged into other activities. Typical of them was Huxley, who asked, 'Why trouble ourselves about matters about which, however important they may be, we know nothing and can know nothing? We live in a world which is full of misery and ignorance, and the plain duty of all of us is to make the little corner he can influence somewhat less miserable and ignorant than it was before he entered it.'

To-day such conflicts are comparatively rare, though by no means unknown,[2] for the religious upbringing which these men had enjoyed is no longer common. But for them the struggle was intense, and when intellectual honesty compelled them to abandon their faith a void was made in their lives which nothing could fill.

It was because religion was so grave a matter that the changing situation produced in many devout souls a feeling almost of panic. There is also a further cause which helps to explain their state of mind; the crisis which confronted them was novel and unforeseen; for the frequent occurrence of similar challenges in the life of the Church had been forgotten. Since the Deist Controversy of the eighteenth century there had been nothing which affected the fundamental truths of Christianity. The disputes which had followed the rise of the Oxford

---

[1] *Contra Gentiles*, IV, 13.
[2] D. H. Lawrence is an instance, of whom T. S. Eliot has written that his vision was spiritual but spiritually sick.

Movement, and what men termed Papal Aggression, had been merely domestic quarrels, now it seemed that religion itself was threatened. To-day we are accustomed to such challenges and to the necessity of making adjustments to meet them; but it was not so in the middle of the nineteenth century. There was then for the average believer a clear-cut line between the acceptance of Christianity in its fullness, and absolute unbelief. Can we wonder that for many whose faith was largely traditional and unexamined it seemed as if the very foundations were being undermined? Moreover, many of the things which troubled them, now seem harmless enough, in the light of our fuller knowledge and different perspective. An acquaintance, for example, with oriental literary methods removes difficulties over Joshua's supposed halting of the sun's course, as also over Balaam's speaking donkey, not to mention Jonah's whale. But these were serious problems a few generations ago, and they still bulk large in open-air propaganda against Christianity.

This sense of crisis was not confined to the ordinary churchgoer, it was also recognized by wiser and better informed observers. In January 1869 Henry Sidgwick wrote: 'I feel convinced that English religious society is going through a great crisis just now, and it will probably become impossible soon to conceal from anybody the the extent to which rationalistic views are held, and the extent of their deviation from traditional opinion.'[1] Westcott, too, in the preface to the third edition of *The Gospel of the Resurrection* published five years later, referred to the common assumption 'that once again we are approaching a great crisis in the history of human society and human thought.'

The new situation certainly presented a challenge to Christianity as generally understood and accepted. But,

[1] *Henry Sidgwick: a Memoir,* p. 187.

as I have said, there was in it nothing that was very novel. All religious systems must from time to time face such challenges; when men begin to inquire into the real meaning and value of beliefs and practices which for long have been taken for granted. Whether they will prove beneficial or otherwise depends upon the manner in which they are handled. Taken wisely they may lead to fuller truth and a growing knowledge of reality; met by unreasoning condemnation they can only result in stagnation and decline. To 'turn back in dismay from the problems which may be the entrance to higher truth . . . to flee before the gale which, rightly faced, might have carried us far on our way, is not of faith, but of unbelief.'[1]

But many, especially among the clergy, had but small suspicion of the severity of the storm which was rapidly moving up. To them these new views were but a cloud on the horizon, which would soon pass, and meanwhile could safely be ignored. The faith as understood and taught by themselves did at least meet the needs of their own flocks, so why make any change? It is a subtle temptation to equate what is found convenient to believe with the truth itself. They forgot those outside, and also that any system which refuses to adjust itself to new truth must ultimately decay, though for a time it may seem to flourish; just as the trunk of a tree may stand long after any hope of blossom or fruit is past, retaining

> The action and the shape without the grace
> Of life.

To them the faith was a firm anchor which could not be disturbed. But though anchors may give a feeling of security they are not conducive to movement, and an anchored vessel may be unable to weather a storm.

[1] Oman, *Vision and Authority*, p. 74.

Such obscurantism failed utterly to comprehend the true nature of the situation. There could be no question of preserving the old exactly as it had been handed down from the past; the only wise course was to accept the new truths and incorporate them in the structure of the faith. 'The broad stream of events,' as Westcott has said, 'cannot be stayed or turned back, but it can be guided along fertilizing channels.'[1] Had the obscurantists prevailed, and in so far as they actually did so, the only outcome would have been a disastrous separation between the Church and the intellectual life of the nation.

Thus the ultra-orthodox took up an attitude of uncompromising opposition to the new knowledge, refusing to surrender even the most untenable of what they regarded as the out-works of the faith, and denouncing those who were prepared to make quite moderate concessions as what we should now call 'fifth columnists.' It was even suggested that the new views had been sent by God to distinguish between the true believers and the rest (cf. I Cor. xi. 19), to make a kind of 'purge' of the Church. Such self-contradictions as were recognized as latent in their conception of Christianity were held to be additional proofs of its verity.

This rigid attitude, which regarded Christianity as a closed system based on an infallible Bible, reveals a strange lack of trust in the guidance of the Holy Spirit;[2] and it is perhaps difficult for us to understand it, for that same Spirit has taught us many lessons of which our fathers were ignorant. To thinkers of a more liberal outlook this type of orthodoxy came, as a consequence, to be regarded as the sin against the Holy Ghost. Its

[1] *The Incarnation and Common Life*, p. 22.
[2] Cf. *Hastings Rashdall*, p. 195: 'To assume that the whole truth is to be found in the decisions of the past is really to disbelieve in the guidance of that Holy Spirit, of Whom it was promised that He should lead Christ's disciples to all truth.'

exponents might keep out the light by drawing down the blinds; but drawn blinds may signify that there has been a death in the house.

Before leaving this question of obscurantism two further remarks are called for. First, it must be understood that ignorance was by no means confined to the defenders of traditional beliefs. John Stuart Mill himself once remarked that 'The future of mankind will be gravely imperilled if great questions are left to be fought out between ignorant change and ignorant opposition to change.'[1] Secondly, that opposition on the part of the traditionalists was by no means confined to the ignorant and unlearned.

The Tractarians were very anxious that no suspicion that the Church of England was departing from the Catholic Faith in its fullness should arise, for this might be the prelude to a new wave of conversions to Rome. Hence their special alarm over the writings of Colenso, who after all was a bishop. But on other grounds the older Anglo-Catholics, as represented by Dr. Pusey and his disciple Liddon, were deeply concerned over the effects which would follow the dissemination of the new views. As early as 1866 the latter had written to Dean Stanley: 'Is not the practical question this—Whether the Church of Christ is to be viewed as a mere Literary Society, or as a home and mother of dying souls.'[2] Liddon, it may be remarked, condemned Stanley as having no logical faculty which would compel him to realize the outcome of his views;[3] but he himself was hampered in his thought by too great a trust in logic. This was pointed out by a friendly critic, Francis Paget, who speaks of him as following 'a single train of thought or inference, pressing

---

[1] Quoted by John Morley, *Recollections*, I, p. 56.
[2] Prothero, *Life and Letters of Dean Stanley*, II, p. 171.
[3] Johnston, *Life and Letters of Henry Parry Liddon*, p. 274.

it without regard to the surrounding facts which tell upon it.' To Lightfoot such a method seemed typical of Oxford thinking as a whole.[1]

Even those theologians who were convinced of the truth of much in the new outlook exercised a considerable economy in their treatment of it and tried to conceal from the public the results reached by German scholars; a procedure which was exposed and condemned by Bishop Thirlwall, as well as by Benjamin Jowett, who saw that it was impossible to keep knowledge at one level in Germany and at another in England. 'The great danger' to him 'was—not lest reason should destroy religion, but lest intellectual persons should reject the truth itself, when stated in grotesque and impossible forms.'[2] It is hard for us to realize the attitude of many of the devout at this epoch. Oman has recorded the shock which he felt, during the Robertson Smith controversy, on being told by a lawyer who was also an elder of the Church that even if Robertson Smith were right and if what he proclaimed was the truth, 'it is a dangerous truth, and he has no right . . . to upset the Church by declaring it.'[3]

But the English people could not be kept behind an iron curtain, and the press and the opponents of Christianity were not slow to popularize views to which the official teachers were either hostile, or concerning which they were reticent.

The ultra-orthodox might be thrown into a panic— Dean Church, with some severity, could say that many of them were behaving 'more like old ladies than philosophers'—and even grave theologians feel vaguely embarrassed by the changing atmosphere of thought, but

---

[1] Paget, *Francis Paget, Bishop of Oxford*, pp. 318f.
[2] Abbott and Campbell, *Life and Letters of Benjamin Jowett*, I, p. 260.
[3] *Vision and Authority*, p. 9.   Cf. the statement on p. 29 below.

for the younger generation the situation was brimming
with joyful promise and hope. 'We threw everything
into the seething pot and wondered what would emerge,'
said Stopford Brooke.[1] Many of them were in a state of
'yeast,' to adopt a term made popular by Charles
Kingsley's novel of that name, and were apt, like the
young and inexperienced in every age, to be scornful of
the old, merely because it was old. This lack of consideration for their elders and for traditional beliefs did
not a little to add to the difficulties of the situation and to
stiffen orthodox opposition. They were, as Stopford
Brooke warned J. R. Green, in too much of a hurry.

Liberal views spread with great rapidity in both
universities, where the influence of J. S. Mill, with his
denunciations of the tame acceptance of tradition, was
predominant. So widespread, indeed, had they become
that when Creighton was ordained in 1870 there was
much adverse comment. He told his wife later, 'that it
was the habit in Oxford to assume that a man who took
Orders must be either a fool or a knave, and that as people
could not call him a fool, they concluded that he must be
a knave.'[2]

Many of the most violent attacks on Christianity came
from those who had once been its adherents. Among the
most active was Leslie Stephen. He had been ordained
priest six months before the appearance of *The Origin of
Species* in 1859, but his faith does not immediately seem
to have been shaken, for in the following year he urged
Ainger to be ordained.[3] In fact it was not until 1875 that
he ceased to be a clergyman. John Morley, another outstanding opponent of orthodoxy, had gone up to Oxford
with the intention of being ordained.[4]

[1] Jacks, *Life and Letters of Stopford Brooke*, p. 628.
[2] *Life and Letters of Mandell Creighton*, I, pp. 75f.
[3] Sichel, *Life of Canon Ainger*, p. 76.
[4] *Recollections*, I, p. 31.

These were perhaps extreme cases, for, as we have seen, many of the laity who felt unable to hold Christianity in its orthodox form still clung to the Church. But for members of the clergy who adopted liberal views the case was more difficult. In actual fact very few relinquished their orders. Leslie Stephen was one of them, and so was Stopford Brooke, who continued to exercise his ministry unconnected with any denomination at Bedford Chapel. Those who remained were frowned upon by the authorities, but kept on their course; Canon Fremantle of Canterbury (later to be Dean of Ripon) even contributed to *The Fortnightly Review*.

Thus the right to hold liberal views, so long as no fundamental article of the faith was denied, was gradually established. An important manifesto of liberal Christianity appeared in October 1865 with the publication of *The Life and Letters of F. W. Robertson*. It came from the pen of Stopford Brooke, an unexpected choice, for he was then a little-known young Irishman who had only recently left college. In the same year E. A. Abbott became Headmaster of the City of London School, and began to produce many theological writings on liberal lines.

If liberal views were spreading in the universities, and if scholars, or some of them, were acquainted with what was being done in Germany, the general public up to the beginning of our period, and, indeed, for a great part of it, were, as we have seen, being kept as far as possible in ignorance of what was happening. But there had been an attempt by certain theologians to break down this conspiracy of silence just before 1860 by the publication of *Essays and Reviews*.[1]

This famous volume had no great intrinsic value, the

---

[1] See further *Religion in the Victorian Era*, pp. 146 ff, and Storr, *The Development of English Theology*, etc., pp. 429 ff.

only really outstanding essay was that of Mark Pattison on 'Tendencies of Religious Thought in England, 1688–1750,' it contained little that was new, and its whole tone and outlook was far too negative to make it a real contribution to theology. The consequences of its publication, however, were enormous. A widespread state of alarm arose and for the moment Evangelicals and Tractarians forgot their differences to join in the outcry against it. There were denunciations from some of the bishops; two of the authors were prosecuted, though unsuccessfully; volumes were written in reply, and in general there was an attempt to crush it by authority. When Frederick Temple, who had contributed the opening essay, was appointed Bishop of Exeter in 1869 the event was described by a High Church journal as 'the darkest crime which had been perpetrated in the English Church.'[1] But not all orthodox Christians agreed in its hasty condemnation. The saintly G. H. Wilkinson, later to become the second Bishop of Truro, welcomed the increased and more intelligent interest in theological questions which it aroused among the laity who had mainly what he described as 'a sort of stupid historical faith, very vague and seldom strengthened by reflection.'[2] Westcott, although he did not approve of the volume, felt that the chief danger was 'a reaction more perilous than scepticism.'[3]

Among new influences which were telling in a liberal direction was the growing knowledge of German theology. Up to 1860 only a few scholars were in touch with what was being done there. The publication of Strauss's *Life of Jesus* in 1835 had shocked many and had perhaps made English theologians over suspicious of

---

[1] Prothero, *Life and Letters of Dean Stanley*, II, p. 372.
[2] Mason, *Memoir of George Howard Wilkinson*, I, p. 82.
[3] *Life and Letters*, I, p. 214.

German productions. But German theologians had much
to teach English scholars, and that not only in the methods
to be adopted. For in Germany theology had a unity and
consistency which was lacking over here; though this
might lead to that typically German fault of forcing facts
into a preconceived scheme, what they themselves call
Tendenz-schriften.

During our period German influences came in with
increasing volume, and by its close, or soon after, they
received a veneration that was excessive; a compensation,
it may be, for the previous state of neglect.

Other influences which would have a decisive effect on
English theology were topical, rather than national or
geographical, and will receive detailed treatment in
subsequent lectures. It will, however, be an advantage at
this point briefly to glance at them and to discuss their
relations with one another.

They can most conveniently be classed under three
heads, each of which, as it happened, is represented by a
publication in the years immediately before 1860. In
1859 there appeared Darwin's *Origin of Species*, and Mill's
On Liberty. In the year previous Buckle had published
his *History of Civilization*. Thus we get our three divi-
sions: science, philosophy, and history. Of the three it
was the last I would venture to suggest that in the long
run proved most disturbing; for it was the rigid application of the new historical methods to the records of
Christianity which above all would revolutionize both
theology and religion.

It is, however, difficult to separate the three influences;
they worked in conjunction. Their united effect, however, was to make a breach with the past wider even than
that made by the Renaissance of the fifteenth and
sixteenth centuries. The latter, after all, was a rebirth,
or claimed to be, a return to Latin studies, and in a much

less degree to Greek.[1] But the new scientific knowledge and the new methods, as they penetrated the life and thought of mankind, involved a complete change of outlook.

The acceptance of the theory of evolution gave to life a sense of continuity which it had hitherto lacked, and at the same time aroused a new interest in the past as an explanation of the present, whilst both past and present were regarded as giving promise for the future; and that future, in view of man's past achievements, was held to contain unlimited prospects of advance. For the Greeks the golden age had lain in the past, and even the Jews knew of a time when the first ancestors of the race dwelt in an earthly Paradise; but traditional Christianity, like later Judaism, looked to the future. In so far, however, as it located that future in another world, or made it depend on the work of Providence, it was repudiated by the ardent minds of the new scientific era. The golden age, for them, was to be realized here on earth, and it would be brought about by man's own efforts wisely directed by reason and the new knowledge.

One effect of this conception of human progress was to subordinate the good of the individual to that of the race. The race was supreme, and to its future welfare he must be prepared to sacrifice himself, or if need be, and this has a sinister ring, to be sacrificed by those in control of the process. But if this outlook has a sinister ring it was not without valuable teaching for an era which had become excessively individualistic, and that not least in its religion. 'History and science, rather than our religion,' wrote Clutton-Brock, 'have taught us, that our fate is not private and individual, but common.'[2]

[1] The influence of the latter has been greatly exaggerated; see my *Erasmus the Reformer*, pp. 4f.
[2] *What is the Kingdom of Heaven?*, p. 80.

Turning to the relations of science, philosophy, and history, it may be said that science, for its part, was a giver rather than a receiver, supplying new facts upon which the rest could work, and, as we have seen, suggesting more exact methods of dealing with facts in general. There grew up, indeed, a school of historians which delighted to call itself scientific. In regard to philosophy it is difficult to make any generalizations, since different schools adopted very different attitudes towards both science and history. The Positivists, for example, looked upon the discoveries of scientists as providing the only reliable form of knowledge, thus basing philosophy upon natural science, as the medieval philosophers had based philosophy and science upon theology. In so doing philosophy unwittingly imposed a form of tyranny on itself and also upon history, for even those who re-pudiated Positivism were often unconsciously affected by its presuppositions. But whilst lauding natural science most philosophers lacked anything like an adequate knowledge of its changing outlook or of the implications which this would involve for their own studies. The laws of causation, for example, were taking on new forms, the conception of relativity was already fore-shadowed, and the concept of mass was being displaced by that of energy.

As to the relations of philosophy and history, many philosophers despised history as merely, in Bosanquet's phrase, 'the doubtful story of successive events.'[1] For them history could only achieve what Plato had called 'opinion' and not knowledge. Philosophy seeks for what is universal and tends to belittle happenings in time and space, but it may forget that if such happenings fail to provide any clue to the nature of the universe—and for many any evidence of Providential guidance—they

[1] *The Principle of Individuality*, etc., p. 79.

do exhibit humanity in action, and thus provide material which the philosopher neglects to his own hurt.

The historian, for his part, is not concerned with the universal, and even the opinions of rival systems are valued by him mainly as illustrating the movement of thought. He wants to know when they emerged, what influence they exerted, and what was their fate. The precise content of their teaching is for him a matter of comparatively little moment.

Although evolution is popularly associated with science alone, the cognate idea of development was permeating both philosophy and history. Truth thus came to be regarded, not as something static and absolute, but as ever growing, as fresh knowledge rose above the horizon. But such an outlook seemed to conflict with the Christian idea of revelation as the act of God and not the discovery of man, a subject to which we shall return in a subsequent lecture.[1] Here it will suffice to point out that the thought of development was an aid to the theologian, for it could be applied to the growth of religion and explain the very different levels of attainment in the Old and New Testaments. The method by which, according to Darwin, evolution worked, that of natural selection, also helped the theologian; for it could be used to meet the criticism that the choice of the Jewish people as recipients of special divine favour was unjust to other nations. Thus science, in the words of A. J. Balfour, 'adopted an idea which has always been an essential part of the Christian view of the Divine economy, and has returned it again to theology, enriched, strengthened and developed.'[2]

From these outside influences theology also reaped other gains. For they provided it with new facts; and once these were established beyond doubt, those who

[1] See below, pp. 55f.
[2] *The Foundations of Belief*, p. 320.

believed that God was the creator and sustainer of the universe were bound to accept them as a fresh revelation of Himself. If such new and enriching knowledge conflicted with much in the Bible that had been held to be divinely revealed, this must be re-examined and, if necessary, rejected as inadequate and as coming from an inferior stage of development. If these influences seem to be purely destructive, further consideration shows that actually this was far from being the case, for they acted as a purifying force, straining out what was unworthy and misleading. In like manner the prophets in ancient Israel had purged the traditional faith from the gross features of a primitive Semitic religion.

Science, philosophy, and history were thus the purgatory of religion, and by removing the things that were shaken left the structure more secure than ever. As my old teacher, Professor Gwatkin, said in his Gifford Lectures, 'science has been a destroying spirit, and has filled the temple of truth with ruins. But the things she has destroyed were only idols. Religion—the highest ideal—she has placed on a firmer throne than ever.'[1]

[1] *The Knowledge of God*, II, p. 278.

Lecture Two

THE IMPACT OF SCIENCE AND PHILOSOPHY

IN England as elsewhere our period was marked by an enormous expansion of scientific knowledge, not only through the accumulation of new facts, but also by the emergence of new theories. Many of the discoveries were due to the introduction of novel or more effective instruments, such as the use of the spectroscope by Stokes and others in astronomy; many to the intense application of the scientific mind to problems which had hitherto baffled it; and the conducting of fresh experiments.

Of new scientific theories in physics, the most important for our purposes was the abandonment of the purely mechanical outlook which derived from Newton. This was mainly due to experiments connected with the phenomena of electro-magnetics and the diffraction of light, begun by Faraday and carried further by Clerk Maxwell in 1864. In biology the cell theory had immense consequences, and even more the work of Charles Darwin to which we shall return. The new geology was also most important for it provided a vast era of time during which evolution could have been at work, in place of the few thousand years which earlier scientists, accepting the received chronology, had had at their disposal. This was demonstrated, for example, in Lyell's *Evidence of the Antiquity of Man*, published in 1863. Towards the close of our period much attention was given to the influences of heredity, following the work of Galton and Weissmann, and culminating in Bateson's revival of the theories of Mendel. The last decade also saw the beginnings of discoveries which were big with consequences for the future, such as Oliver Lodge's experiments with wireless waves, the work of William Crookes on X-rays, and that of J. J. Thomson on electrons.

So great was the flood of new knowledge that men were almost staggered by it; and Bishop Burroughs, in whose memory these lectures are delivered, once rather whimsically suggested that there should be a pause in discovery so that what was already known might be assimilated. A suggestion which reminds one of Cotter Morison's reaction to the problem of over-population: 'If only the devastating torrent of children could be arrested for a few years, it would bring untold relief.'

Although Darwin published *The Origin of Species* in 1859 its effects were not immediately realized and, in fact, the appearance of *The Descent of Man* twelve years later was a much greater shock to the orthodox. The idea of evolution had long been current; Darwin's contribution was to suggest a theory as to how it worked in biology, what he called natural selection. Those organisms which adapted themselves to their environment survived, those which failed to do so perished. Although Darwin maintained that 'Natural Selection works solely by and for the good of each being,'[1] the general impression it left was one of 'nature red in tooth and claw.' It was also open to the criticism that those best fitted to survive might not of necessity be the highest and best—the rather unfair example of a man meeting a tiger in a jungle was given as an instance.

The controversy provoked by *The Origin of Species* attracted wide attention; in part, because Darwin wrote in a style which the average man could understand; in part, because of the supposed implications for religion.

[1] *The Origin of Species*, p. 428.

It is this latter aspect which has persisted, and it is often cited, by those who should know better, as a classic example of theological obscurantism. In actual fact the main opposition, as Darwin himself had anticipated, came from scientists.[1] Churchmen such as Samuel Wilberforce can hardly be blamed for accepting the prevailing opinion of men of science and so condemning a novel theory. In 1860, as Huxley has testified, 'the supporters of Mr. Darwin's views . . . were numerically extremely insignificant.'[2]

When Darwin was asked by Tennyson whether his theories told against Christianity, he replied, 'No, certainly not.'[3] What they did was to destroy the old teleology which had tried to establish the wisdom and goodness of God from nature, regarded as a machine. When it was viewed no longer as a machine, but as an organism, the argument from design based on its utility lost force; but the idea of purpose in the universe was really deepened and widened. Darwin himself wrote in 1873: 'The impossibility of conceiving that this great and wondrous universe arose through chance seems to me the chief argument for the existence of God.' After all, evolution merely attempts to explain a process; 'why there has been any evolution at all, and why it has taken a spiritual direction, evolutionary science is not competent to say.'[4]

But if those competent to assess the situation saw in evolution no threat to religion, its effects on the general public were disastrous. Men hailed it as a new gospel and saw in its working the assurance of unending progress.

[1] See Raven, *Science, Religion and the Future*, pp. 35ff. and cf. Morley, *Recollections*, I, p. 13: 'One group of scientific men fought another group over the origin of species.'

[2] *Life of Charles Darwin*, II, p. 186.

[3] *Memoir of Alfred, Lord Tennyson*, II, p. 57. The debt owed to Darwin for his courageous adherence to theistic views was acknowledged by Liddon (*Life and Letters*, p. 276).   [4] Storr, *The Living God*, p. 60.

Thus the ground was being prepared for a sort of religion of nature which in a few generations entirely displaced Christianity for a large part of mankind. Such was the opinion of William James.[1]

Evolution was welcomed by some of the more extreme liberals as freeing man from the tyranny of religion; the very idea of God, it was hoped, would soon disappear, so Swinburne proclaimed in *Hertha*:

> Thought made him and breaks him,
>   Truth slays and forgives;
> But to you, as time takes him,
>   This new thing it gives,
> Even love . . . that feeds upon freedom and lives.

Little did he realize to what 'liberation' was to lead, or imagine the even worse tyrannies which were coming upon mankind.[2]

The discoveries of the nineteenth century, however, seem to degrade rather than exalt humanity. Copernicus had dethroned man's dwelling-place from being the centre of the universe, now man himself was shown to be, so far as his body was concerned, nothing more than a part of the natural process and akin to the beasts around him. The claim of Genesis that he was a special creation could no longer be maintained. If man's spiritual nature was of like character, or merely imaginary, then he did, indeed, suffer a still further and final degradation. This Bacon had long ago foreseen, saying of man, 'if he be not kin to God by his spirit he is an ignoble creature.'[3] Liberal thinkers, however, were not troubled—and they were right—by man's humble origins; what mattered was his present exaltation. 'We have little to learn of

---

[1] *Varieties of Religious Experience*, p. 91.

[2] There was something to be said for his attitude for it can hardly be denied that religion was being used to bolster up the prevailing social system. This is the explanation of the anti-religious Socialism of the Continent and of present-day Communism.   [3] Essay *On Atheism*.

apes,' wrote George Meredith with lofty scorn, 'and they may be left.'[1]

But the change in man's status is perhaps not so great after all, for as the latest product of evolution he is still the crown of creation as known to himself; and even if the earth is no longer the centre of the universe the practical difference is negligible. The real significance of things depends, not on bulk or station, but on intellectual and spiritual qualities.

Science had certainly great achievements to its credit, for it was a creator as well as a discoverer, and in a comparatively short space had not only altered the outlook of educated men and women, but had also revolutionized social and economic life. It is no marvel therefore if some scientists calmly assumed that its methods and findings would never again be challenged, or that W. K. Clifford could even identify the advancement of scientific thought with human progress itself. We escaped by a small margin the setting up of a new orthodoxy based on science, having as its Aquinas the venerable figure of Mr. Herbert Spencer.

What is, however, remarkable is that scientists, who would have shrunk with horror from dogmatizing in those departments of science which were not their special province, did not hesitate to make pronouncements upon metaphysics and theology where their knowledge was even more scanty. Tyndall in his presidential address to the British Association in 1871 made an attack on orthodoxy which exposed him to much ridicule. He confessed that his knowledge of primitive religions did not go beyond what was contained in a few popular text-books, whilst his views on history had been abandoned fifty years before. His ignorance was made plain in an amusing

---

[1] *The Egoist*, p. 2. In *Diana of the Crossways*, p. 14, however, he refers to the 'unfailing aboriginal democratic old monster that waits to pull us down.'

article by Robertson Smith. A more serious reply came from two eminent scientists, Professors Tait and Balfour Smith, in a volume entitled *The Unseen Universe*, in which they argued that religion and science, far from being opposed, were really upholding similar conclusions—the existence of a transcendental universe and the immortality of the soul.[1]

Thus whilst science was felt to be a living light among 'the watch-fires of the world,' some of its exponents, exasperated by what they regarded as perverse opposition, were not content to 'lift the torch of reason in the dusky cave of life,' but thrust their smoking brands in the faces of their opponents. This, however, was not the consistent attitude of the greater men; much though they might resent the refusal to accept views which to them seemed so obvious and incontrovertible. Too great an absorption might blind them to the value of spiritual things, and of much else that gives real meaning to life, as Darwin ruefully admitted,[2] none the less they were not prepared to confine reality to the material world. 'God and spirit I know,' said Tyndall, 'and matter I know, and I believe in both.'[3] Even the redoubtable Huxley, regarded by many as the chief protagonist of the scientific view of life, proclaimed that 'The antagonism of Science is not to Religion, but to the heathen survivals and bad philosophy under which Religion herself is well-nigh crushed." He also declared in his Romanes Lecture for 1893 that the higher life of man was in no way due to natural evolution, but rather the result of man's fight against it. Even Herbert Spencer wished to retain some form of religion as a corrective of mere Naturalism.

---

[1] This volume, originally published anonymously, exercised great influence, though now quite forgotten. See Black and Chrystal, *W. Robertson Smith*, pp. 161 ff.

[2] *Life*, I, pp. 102 f.

[3] *Memoir of Alfred, Lord Tennyson*, II, p. 380.

Scientists might condemn their opponents as obscurantists, but they somehow forgot that science itself is based on assumptions which cannot be proved. The claim for example that like causes will always produce like effects may be true of the past, but who can say that it will hold good of the future? Scientists, moreover, show nervousness when confronted with claims that seem to conflict with their preconceived ideas. The case of telepathy is an instance of this. A leading biologist once said to William James that even if it were true, 'scientists ought to band together to keep it suppressed and concealed. It would undo the uniformity of nature, and all sorts of things without which scientists cannot carry on their pursuits.'[1]

Furthermore, although science had made wonderful discoveries it had no answer to give to the riddle of the universe. None the less its prestige ranked very high with the multitude, who did not worry about such high matters, and were impressed with the ability of science to provide means for material betterment. There was as yet no suspicion of the immense harm which would follow scientific discoveries and the destructive use which might be made of them—the atom-bomb and chemical and bacteriological warfare lay in the hidden future.

But science was not everywhere so highly regarded. In the academic world it was looked upon as an upstart— the public schools and the universities were still largely under clerical control; and scholars knew, as the general public did not, that science itself spoke with a divided voice. People talked glibly of 'science' as if it were a single whole, and did not realize its immense complexity and the difficulty of obtaining even a working knowledge of its various branches. Science, too, had its critics among those who were far from orthodox Christians. Carlyle

[1] *The Will to Believe*, p. 10. Cf. p. 14 above.

once said that 'If Adam had remained in Paradise there had been no anatomy and no metaphysics.'

These different attitudes to science must be borne carefully in mind when we attempt to survey the effects of scientific discoveries, for their impact on popular religion was very different from their impact on theology.

Popular religion received definite harm from the progress of science, which added to the general uncertainty of the times, especially as demonstrating that the Bible was not all that had been claimed for it. For the more thoughtful it led to a magnification of the natural order; even some of the orthodox were tempted to find in nature the only representation of God to which man could attain. But perhaps the most serious harm came indirectly, in so far as science led to a trust in material things and a greater dependence on the comforts of life.

The progress of science also raised many problems for the theologian; though if he were sufficiently wise he would recognize that even if much in the Bible had been shaken its real value as concerned with the relations of God to man, and man to man, had been unaffected, or even enriched. But his task was heavy and arduous, for he had not only to attempt to assimilate a multitude of new facts, but also to adjust his ideas to an entirely new way of looking at things. Christian beliefs had been formulated in an age which held a geocentric theory of the universe, and certain of them, such as our Lord's visible Ascension and the conception of a local heaven 'above the bright blue sky,' were clearly incompatible with the new knowledge. But, as we saw in the previous lecture, science was useful to the theologian in a variety of ways. A further benefit was that it helped to correct the over-emphasis on the transcendence of God to which theology had been prone by showing that He was still active in the world.

The difficulties aroused by science were met in various ways. The Roman Church had its cut and dried methods, and the Vatican Council of 1870, the same which recognized papal infallibility, anathematized anyone who said that 'the doctrines of the Church can ever receive a sense in accordance with the progress of science other than that which the Church has understood and still understands.'

Those who were more favourably disposed towards scientific discoveries made much of the gaps in our knowledge which science had failed to fill—some have since been bridged or reduced—and, by a kind of inverted agnosticism, tried to buttress their faith with ignorance rather than knowledge; an attitude of mind which, if logically pressed, would dread rather than welcome new discoveries, and was scarcely worthy of those who professed to be followers of Him who declared that He was the Truth.

At the same time Christian thinkers were justified in maintaining a certain reserve; for the conclusions of science were based 'on inquiries which left vast areas of life unexplained and even unexplored.'[1] Science, moreover, finds supreme significance in the cosmic and general and takes little account of the experiences of the individual. Yet these too are 'facts' in the fullest meaning of the term. Illingworth cited the effect of a sunset or a piece of music as examples of 'impressions which profoundly touch the feelings, and modify the conduct of innumerable men'; and argued that such impressions 'may even be called more real . . . than their mechanical causes.'[2] There was also a growing suspicion that scientific discoveries, which in their early days had given men a sense of freedom and expansion, would in the long run tell against them. The uniformity of nature might prove a burden, and man

[1] Major, *Life of W. Boyd Carpenter*, p. 149.
[2] *Divine Immanence*, pp. 55f.

find himself trapped in a ruthless scheme of things. The Christian mind was especially revolted by what seemed like a deification of natural law and causal uniformity.

Between genuine science and genuine theology, however, there can be no real opposition; for both have to do with the world which God has made. The discoveries of science, once they are established—and this is often a less certain process than is sometimes thought[1]—must be accepted by the theologian. At the same time the scientist for his part must not hastily set aside the religious sentiments of the human heart as unworthy of consideration, much less dismiss them as 'survivals' which will one day disappear.

The conflicts between science and religion which occurred in the nineteenth century were due in the main to misunderstandings, and the failure of both science and religion to appreciate the position of the other. There was also a natural tendency to take extreme utterances, on the one side as on the other, as typical and representative. Science and religion alike had to recognize their different spheres. But this is no easy matter, for as in the case of the Empire and the Papacy in the Middle Ages, such spheres undoubtedly overlap and exactly to define their limits is beyond human ingenuity.

Some of the attempts to reconcile religion and science were undoubtedly premature, and some delusive. As with many so-called understandings in politics, both international and domestic, they were often based on formulas which each side took in a different sense. Jowett foretold that any final reconciliation would only take place when religion was 'enlightened, extended and purified, and philosophy and science inspired and

---

[1] Many scientific 'articles of faith,' such as the universal ether and the absolute conservation of matter and of energy, have either been abandoned or considerably modified.

elevated, and both allied together in the service of God and man.'[1]

Jowett's conjunction of philosophy and science brings us to the second part of our subject—the impact of philosophy. As we saw in the first lecture, science and philosophy were by no means in entire agreement. Both were tending to become more self-sufficient, an unfortunate consequence of over-specialization and the multiplication of technical terms which rendered each more incomprehensible to the other.

Though some philosophers welcomed the results and methods of natural science, others more or less ignored it as incapable of contributing to the knowledge of reality. Science confined its interests to the world of phenomena and neglected matters which were vital for philosophy. 'It cannot be a matter of unconcern,' wrote A. K. Rogers, 'whether reality . . . is something which justifies and backs up those interests which we recognize as highest in human life or whether the latter are but the unessential incident upon the surface of a universe which, at its heart, is quite indifferent to them.'[2] Science, in a word, failed to give any intelligible account of the universe as a whole.

Differences between science and philosophy led a number of leading minds to join together for the purpose of examining them and so the Metaphysical Society was founded in 1869. Among its members were not only philosophers such as Sidgwick, W. G. Ward, and Martineau, and scientists such as Huxley, Tyndall, and Clifford, but also ecclesiastics like Cardinal Manning and Archbishop Thomson of York, men of letters like Tennyson, Ruskin, and Leslie Stephen, and even politicians such as Gladstone and Morley.[3] If its meetings

---

[1] *Sermons on the Faith of Darwin*, pp. 20ff.
[2] *Modern Philosophy*, p. 229.
[3] See further A. W. Brown, *The Metaphysical Society: Victorian Minds in Crisis, 1869–80.*

D

found no solutions to the various problems involved, they did at least bring men of differing views together and helped to remove misunderstandings and bitterness. They also served to arouse a new interest in metaphysics, and for those who could no longer accept the Christian scheme of life they disclosed the need for finding a fresh and stable foundation for ethics.

We turn now to a brief survey of the various systems of philosophy which were prominent in our period, especially as they affected theology.

The prevailing system at its beginning was Utilitarianism, a somewhat bleak and uninspiring theory of the meaning of life which does little to encourage the higher desires of mankind. In it everything exists for the sake of something else; art for edification, knowledge for use. It has no absolute values and no joy in the passing moment.[1] And this in spite of its expressed anxiety to promote the happiness, harmony, and comfort of humanity; a process which largely consisted in freeing it from the restraints of tradition, especially as this was enshrined in religious beliefs. Its limitations were recognized, late in life, by John Stuart Mill, who had been its chief exponent, and the publication of his posthumous essay on *Theism* in 1870 aroused something like dismay in his disciples, and made 'a sort of intellectual scandal.'[2] Mill came to perceive that mankind needs some form of religion, and though in *Theism* he accepted the view that creation reveals an intelligent mind at work, previously he had commended the Comtist 'religion of humanity.'

Comte had died in 1857, but he left behind him in England a small but influential body of followers which included Frederic Harrison, E. S. Beesly, and J. H.

[1] Cf. Jacks, *Life and Letters of Stopford Brooke*, p. 582.
[2] Morley, *Recollections*, I, p. 106. See further Storr, *Development of English Theology*, etc., pp. 392ff.

Bridges. They held meetings in Fetter Lane for the worship of humanity, where it was said that there were three persons and no God. Positivism, although its social teaching influenced Westcott and others, was too artificial a system to carry much weight, and Huxley summed it up in a damning phrase as 'Catholicism minus Christianity.' Its chief value was the testimony which it bore to the existence of man's need for religion, even if it denied the possibility of metaphysics; but like Utilitarianism its only service to theology was the negative one of challenging theologians to re-examine their presuppositions and fundamental beliefs. Incidentally it was Frederic Harrison who first brought *Essays and Reviews* to the notice of the educated public.

A great and astonishing influence during most of our period was that of Herbert Spencer, though by the end of the century his system was as good as dead. Why it appealed so strongly to many thoughtful people, apart from trained philosophers, is hard to explain. It did, however, offer an ordered set of beliefs which could be directly applied to life, and took account of the changed opinion of the times; it was also of a highly optimistic character. Perhaps Spencer's most useful service was to recognize the limitations of our knowledge, though this did not lead him to appreciate the need for a divine revelation.

All these systems were too critical and destructive, too narrowly intellectual, to provide for the deeper needs of humanity. It is not therefore surprising that a reaction in favour of Idealism began to take place. Such a reaction had already occurred in Germany with Hegel, and had had a profound influence on theologians. Through them it had spread to England. 'Our theological outlook to-day,' Storr has claimed, 'is what it is, largely because this philosophical development took place.'[1]

[1] *Op. cit.*, p. 199.

For our purposes the great services of Hegel were to bring the historical element into the philosophy of religion and to apply to theology itself the idea of development. His chief influence was in relation to dogmatic theology, and therein to Christology above all, for it was because his theories proved unacceptable that further work was stimulated on the problem of the relation between the historical Jesus and the Christ of dogma. Hegel, who was a Lutheran, looked upon his work as a defence of orthodox Christianity; but many regarded it in a far different light. He had died in 1831 and his philosophy had already lost influence in Germany when it was being welcomed elsewhere.[1]

The most influential exponent of Idealism in England was T. H. Green. 'He it was,' wrote Scott Holland, 'who shook us all free from the bondage of cramping philosophies and sent us out once again on the high pilgrimage towards Ideal Truth.'[2] Green is sometimes regarded as a disciple of Hegel whom he had studied in his younger days. But later he had drawn away from him, mainly under the influence of Lotze.[3] He was a strong opponent of the shallow agnosticism which flourished in his day; and was also most insistent on the self-sufficiency of the moral ideal, which in his eyes required no reinforcing by the offer of rewards or the threat of punishment. At the same time he recognized to the full the part which religion must play in upholding morality.

Although Green exercised considerable influence in Oxford it was neither so extensive or so persistent as that of Mill. This may have been due in part to his comparatively early death and that of his chief disciple, R. L.

---

[1] 'There is no doubt that Hegelianism is on the increase—everywhere except in Germany,' wrote Sidgwick in 1870 (*Memoir*, p. 230).

[2] *A Bundle of Memories*, p. 145.

[3] Nettleship, *Thomas Hill Green: a Memoir*, p. 192; cf. p. 126 note.

Nettleship.[1] But if his influence on philosophical thought was by no means unchallenged, his influence on theology was profound. This came about through the acceptance of his teaching by a group of Oxford Anglicans, the group from which *Lux Mundi* would later emerge.

This group was almost unique in English theology as possessing a philosophical basis. England was very different from Germany where philosophy and theology went hand in hand, as in the case of the Tübingen school and Hegel. Another German philosopher who influenced theology was Ritschl who died in 1889 at the age of 67. In early life he had been a disciple of Hegel but like most of his contemporaries in Germany he reacted towards Kant, and was also affected by Schleiermacher. The principal idea in his system was the exaltation of 'values' at the expense of 'facts.' He strongly insisted, however, on the historicity of Jesus and on the importance of His teaching; he held, indeed, that through Christ alone was God revealed to man. This led to a depreciation of the Old Testament and to the denial of any contribution from non-Christian religions. But though he accepted a divine revelation he refused to recognize any supernatural character in the records of that revelation; a position which was held by Robertson Smith in this country. The followers of Ritschl diverged considerably from the ideas of their master; the best known of them, Harnack, was by no means the most typical. In the last decade of the nineteenth century the views of Ritschl aroused some attention over here.[2]

The Ritschlians, whilst emphasizing the subjective elements in religion and distrusting metaphysics, clung

---

[1] Bosanquet and F. H. Bradley, who may be regarded as carrying on the same tradition, exercised little influence in Oxford, though the latter made his home there.

[2] See J. Orr, *The Ritschlian Theology and the Evangelical Faith* (1898), and A. E. Garvie, *The Ritschlian Theology* (1899).

tenaciously to the historic Christ. This could not be
affirmed of the Pragmatists who were disdainful of
historic facts and brought all ideas to the test of whether
they 'worked' or not. Thus truth was subordinated to
practice. Somewhat similar views were held by the
French Roman Catholic Modernists who accepted the
Church as an effective organization, but regarded the
truth or falsehood of the events upon which its claims
were based as a matter of little consequence.

We saw above that Idealism in Oxford never attained
an unchallenged position. As early as 1870 there was a
reaction from it led by Thomas Case, a movement which
gathered force in the remainder of our period, though it
was not until the beginning of the present century that it
became fully active with the publication by the Cambridge philosopher, G. E. Moore, of *The Refutation of
Idealism*. It may be noted that both Realists and Idealists
accepted the theory of evolution, but their attitude towards it was very different. The former were interested
only in the process, explaining man's development in
terms of nature; the latter laid emphasis on the end
towards which evolution was working, an end which
they regarded as spiritual. The main criticism of Idealism
was that it was too speculative, and also that it tended to
belittle personality. In any case Idealists, so their opponents alleged, were attempting a premature synthesis,
before the necessary facts were available.

One striking feature of the thought of the closing years
of our period was an immense growth of what may be
called Humanism, that theory of life which makes man
the measure of all things and the centre of the universe.
Its rise may not be unconnected with the breaking down
of the old notions which had given so exalted a position
to man and his little earth. Humanism, in this case, was
man's assertion of his continued significance. Since man

THE IMPACT OF SCIENCE AND OF PHILOSOPHY 39

is capable of working out his own destiny and even of controlling nature, there is no need to bring in the idea of God or Providence; in fact, such an idea is a delusion, and where fostered may stand in the way of human progress. This was the teaching of Karl Marx, and to-day it is largely the unconscious creed of much of Western civilization, opposed though it is to Communism. What its future may be is hard to say, for Humanism has some obvious weaknesses. Not only does it rob man of God, but it also takes away his worth as an individual. Furthermore it seems to be a philosophy best fitted for an age of prosperity and may find it difficult to survive in less happy days. The most damaging criticism, however, is that its fundamental assumptions are open to question. Recent experience tends to show that the more man extends his sway over nature, the less is he able to control mental forces.

Humanism found an extreme exponent in Nietzsche who regarded the progress of mankind as bound up with the elimination of the weak and unfit; so only could a race of supermen eventually emerge. Christian morality he derided as fit only for slaves.

We come now to a consideration of the relations of philosophy and theology. Though both deal with much the same problems and have as their objective a description of reality as a whole their approach is different. Theology is bound up with religion and attaches a much greater importance to the imagination and the emotions than does philosophy, which tends to be purely intellectual. Religion, too, demands a personal object; whereas philosophy in its effort to unify knowledge is unconcerned as to whether the basis of such unity is personal or not. For those who cannot accept any explanation of the universe which does not provide for relationship between God and man philosophy can never be enough. This was the attitude of T. H. Green who wrote to Scott Holland in 1872: 'I never dreamt of philosophy doing instead of religion. My own interest in it, I believe, is wholly religious; in the sense that it is to me . . . the reasoned intellectual expression of the effort to get to God.'[1]

Another important difference between them is that theology claims to be based on a divine revelation. Incidentally this perhaps explains the neglect of philosophy by most English theologians. Such a claim is not without its dangers for it may render theology unnatural and artificial by cutting it off from secular knowledge. It revives the old medieval conflict between the Nominalists and Realists (not to be confused with those who now bear this name) as to whether thought should be restricted to an ideal world or whether reality should be sought in the world around.

There was also another danger in so far as too great a dependence on a supposed revelation may lead to rigidity and the conservation of obsolete traditions. To the philosopher the theologian was no disinterested seeker after truth, but the apologist of a dogmatic system who deliberately ignored fresh facts and would not admit the need for restatement in the light of growing knowledge.[2]

Such a criticism, however, did not apply to all theologians, for many of them realized the need for an intellectual statement and vindication of Christian belief. Christianity could not be allowed to find its sole basis in the emotions, or even in the pronouncements of an authoritative Church. It is not enough for a Christian to have 'a blind faith for which he can give no better reason

---

[1] Quoted Paget, *Henry Scott Holland*, p. 65.

[2] 'Religion is not the highest form of truth, even though the truth which it reveals is substantially the highest and final truth. Its message is formally imperfect, tainted by the displacement of assertion from the truth to the symbol.' Collingwood, *Speculum Mentis*, p. 145.

than that it makes him comfortable to hold it, or that he has been ordered to hold it by some authority into whose trustworthiness it is forbidden to inquire.'[1]

There is thus a need for a philosophy of religion, a system in which due place is given to religious experience, to feeling and intuition; but before these are accepted as guides they must justify themselves at the bar of reason. This, as Hastings Rashdall has observed, was 'the spirit of that noble band, the Cambridge Platonists,' and, he adds, 'is the spirit which we want to see rekindled in our schools of theology.'[2] In a word any really profound theology must have philosophical outworks and be willing to submit itself to philosophical criticism. In the same way a really sound metaphysic must have a firm theological centre.[3] But every religion, it may be urged, even the most primitive, has already some kind of a metaphysic, either conscious or unconscious. That is true; but what is required is the formal expression of a metaphysic. Religion, even when based on a revelation, cannot by itself achieve this.[4] 'Christian theology,' wrote Canon Storr, 'cannot satisfactorily create its own metaphysic. It must call in the aid of philosophy for the task. A theology which seeks its material only in the revelation contained in the Bible will both fail to understand that material itself and will make the part the standard for interpreting the whole.'[5]

Theology, then, is defective unless the religious experiences which lie behind it are tested by reason. But

[1] A. E. Taylor in *Essays Catholic and Critical*, p. 31.

[2] *Principles and Precepts*, p. 211.

[3] J. R. Illingworth as a young man deplored the habit of rushing straight at theology without any consideration of the philosophical outworks; just as later he saw that there could be no new metaphysic unless there was a firm grasp of the theological core. *Life*, pp. 36 and 160.

[4] 'Buddhism is a metaphysic which gave birth to a religion—Christianity is a religion vainly seeking a metaphysic.' Whitehead, *Religion in the Making*, pp. 39f.

[5] *The Development of English Theology*, etc., p. 14.

what is reason? The term is really very vague, and in practice it often means no more than the philosophical outlook which is predominant at any particular time. If theology, therefore, becomes unduly subservient to reason it may find itself, as in Germany, too closely attached to one philosophical system. But if theology is to express its message in a form which will appeal to contemporary thought this cannot entirely be avoided. 'Theology must sometimes,' as Dr. Tennant has said, 'deliberately take over ready-fashioned concepts from philosophy . . . and the theology of any particular generation can hardly avoid using, unconsciously if not with full awareness, the ideas and beliefs of contemporary science, and allowing them to mould its exegesis and its doctrine.'

Reason, however we interpret the term, has, of course, its very serious limitations. It is, for one thing, incapable of taking those flights into the sublime which are possible to insight and intuition, for 'the finite intellect cannot transcend the conditions of finitude.' Its beneficial functions, indeed, are largely negative, consisting in the rejection of fanciful and unworthy ideas. But if applied too strictly it may provoke a reaction in the direction of superstition, for if religion becomes over-intellectual it may cease to provide for the spiritual needs of the many. Offered stones when they demand bread, they may even turn to the husks on which the swine are fed. It is certainly possible to exalt reason too highly—Herbert Spencer once complained that it was made a kind of idol—but to neglect or depreciate it is blameworthy, for such a policy is in reality the evasion of problems rather than an attempt to solve them.

There were not lacking in our period a number of philosophers who, accepting the Christian point of view, tried to work out a philosophy of religion which would be in accord with the thought of the day. Like other philosophers they held different opinions on a number of points; Hastings Rashdall, not the least able of them, was, for example, a determinist. Some of them were amateurs, such as A. J. Balfour, whose *Foundations of Belief* was published in 1895.

The most influential group was, however, that already referred to as disciples of T. H. Green. The alliance of this group with Idealism was undoubtedly useful in its beginnings as offering resistance to stark Naturalism; but by the end of the century the utility of the connexion was open to question. Alliances, we know, are good up to a point; but if the ultimate, as distinguished from the immediate, aims of the allies are divergent, they lose their meaning. The great problem for these Christian Idealists was the exact relation of God and the Absolute,[1] and some of them accepted perhaps too eagerly a philosophy which was overwhelmingly immanentist. Gore was here an exception owing to his vivid awareness of moral distinctions. This emphasis on immanence, of course, fitted in well with the Logos theology, and seemed to give room for the recognition of the divine purpose in history; but it neglected much that was fundamental in the Christian tradition as contained in the Bible, and in earlier thinkers, not to mention the liturgy.

Outstanding among Christian philosophers on account of his ability to make himself popularly understood was J. R. Illingworth. His works had an immense sale, appearing in cheap paper-backed editions and being translated into many languages, including Chinese and Japanese. Most of them appeared after 1900; but in our period, in addition to two essays in *Lux Mundi*, he published his Bampton Lectures on *Personality: Human and*

[1] Both Bradley and Bosanquet denied personality in the Absolute: C. C. J. Webb, *Religious Thought in England*, etc., p. 48.

Divine and also *Divine Immanence*. Illingworth's contribution to thought was hampered by the retired life which he lived and by his inability to afford to buy the newest books. This kept him ignorant of modern developments; but apart from this, like other members of the *Lux Mundi* set, having made considerable progress in a liberal direction, in later life he refused to advance any further.

One admirable characteristic of these Christian philosophers was their attitude to reason. They were genuine rationalists, for they gave to reason its proper place, while recognizing its limitations. On the one hand they did not despise what lay below it, and on the other they did not ignore what lay beyond.

Finally we have to ask ourselves what were the effects of philosophy on religion. We have already, in discussing the place of reason, seen that it helped to reject elements in the popular religion which were fanciful and unworthy. But this was a negative tendency and by some exponents it was over-emphasized and only added to the general unsettlement. Liddon in 1868 went so far as to claim that the prevalence of the views of Mill, Bain, and Herbert Spencer made impossible all serious theology in Oxford since they denied the first and highest theistic truths.[1] None the less philosophy rendered great services to theology in providing it with new categories or conceptions for the work of interpretation, as well as systems based on human thought which could be set alongside dogmas based on revelation. By bringing their conclusions to the test of such systems theologians were enabled to discard from them what was merely local or accidental. On the more positive side philosophy helped towards that unification of knowledge which it shares as a common aim with theology.

[1] Johnston, *Life and Letters of H. P. Liddon*, p. 113.

Lecture Three

THE IMPACT OF HISTORICAL STUDIES :
BIBLICAL CRITICISM

THE second half of the nineteenth century saw a revival of interest in history in England. During the restoration period and until 1730 England had possessed a notable school of medieval historians,[1] but then for more than a century history came to be despised and neglected, in spite of a few great names such as Gibbon and Macaulay. The revival in the second half of the nineteenth century was due, at least in part, to the work of Darwin, for it revealed nature working out its development in time. Before that the accepted view had been that organisms were permanently divided into different kinds; a view which led Hegel to deny that nature had any history. The new scientific influence was not, however, without its drawbacks, for it led to the application of 'evolution' to spheres to which it did not rightly belong; 'the crude transference of the evolutionary hypotheses to the conduct of human affairs,' for example, did much harm;[2] and in general it suggested that to trace out the development of an idea or institution was sufficient to explain it.

In the past history had been the work of amateurs and had formed part of general literature. Henceforward, as the subject came to be increasingly studied in the universities, it would be more and more restricted to

[1] See D. C. Douglas, *English Scholars.*
[2] Cf. *Life and Letters of Mandell Creighton,* II, p. 469.

professionals; in fact the study of history was turned into a vast co-operative enterprise, the virtual monopoly of dons and their pupils. This was largely the result of German influence to which the new school of historians, led by Stubbs, was greatly indebted. It flourished first at Oxford for it was not until Creighton became the first Dixie Professor of Ecclesiastical History at Cambridge in 1884 that the new methods can be said to have been introduced there.

The new school, following the maxim of Ranke that the facts are all-important, tended to concentrate on the study of details. The older historians, whose object was primarily to construct from their authorities a narrative which was at once picturesque and enlightening, would have scoffed at this as mere learned trifling. But they themselves had been deficient in critical ability and unable to consult more than a restricted range of documents. As a result they had accepted as true much that was mere legend or propaganda. Under the minute scrutiny of intensive research this was exposed and denounced. In consequence the impression gained ground that the new historians were bent only on destruction. The American humorist, Artemus Ward, put the popular opinion very succinctly when he wrote: 'The researches of many eminent antiquarians have already thrown much darkness on the subject; and it is possible, if they continue their labours, that we shall soon know nothing at all.' But such a stage was necessary if secure foundations were to be laid for future advance. The too exclusive emphasis on the collection of facts, however, was a real weakness in Victorian historical scholarship; for it was not sufficiently counterbalanced by the gift of imagination. Facts became almost an end in themselves, and though they are necessary as a basis for a true appreciation of any situation or development, even more necessary is the ability to judge which are the really significant facts. Facts, in other words, are the raw material of history, not history itself. R. G. Collingwood, a redoubtable critic of the Victorian conception of the writing of history, went so far as to affirm that 'Nothing capable of being memorized is history.'

Anticipations of the newer attitude to the writing of history are to be found in *The New Republic*, that remarkable *tour de force* of an Oxford undergraduate, W. H. Mallock, published in 1877. In it he says, 'The least important of all the world's events are those that you can localize exactly, and put an exact date to; those alone which most historians see . . . events . . . I call *illustrations* of history; but I do not call them history.' And again, 'Our past must be an extension of the present, or it is no real past.'[1]

If history owed some of its restored prestige to the work of scientists it was also indebted to them for improved methods. But in adopting scientific rules for weighing evidence historians did not always realize the immense difference between their own studies and those of scientists. The scientist can either reproduce the objects he studies, as in chemistry, or observe them afresh, as in astronomy; this the historian cannot do, save only in his own consciousness. There is a further difference of equal importance; events in nature are events and nothing more, events in history are the products of human agency.

As history became more scientific and more given up to the collection of facts, it was avid of fresh material on which to work. So libraries were searched for forgotten documents, and the earth itself for the remnants of lost civilizations. From the latter sources there came an enormous influx of new knowledge, and discoveries

[1] *Op. cit.*, Bk. III, ch. ii (1908 edn., p. 131).

followed one another in an almost breathless succession.[1] Forgotten peoples sprang suddenly to life and much that had been unknown to the Greeks themselves of their own not too distant past was made available for scholars. In 1874 Schliemann revealed the antiquities of Troy; then came the discovery of the Minoan civilization; and from Egyptian dust-heaps fragments of lost dramatists and Aristotle's *Constitution of Athens*. Assyria and Babylon too were yielding up their treasures to the enriching of Old Testament studies. It was in 1876 that George Smith published the Creation and Deluge tablets from Nineveh.

Archaeology thus provided new material, and, what should not be ignored, much of it material of a quite different kind from that previously available. Hitherto historians had had to rely on written authorities, now they had material which had actually come down from the past. At the same time it must be realized that much that is discovered by excavation is only fragmentary and has survived by accident. Its importance must not be unduly exaggerated.

One effect of all these discoveries was to bring a new idea of the vastness and extent of human achievement. This reinforced the optimistic outlook of the times; though by the end of the century it was beginning to be realized that since progress had been neither uniform nor uninterrupted the fate which had come upon the great civilizations of the past might perchance befall our own. The pushing back of the horizon of history and the immense increase of the span of human life upon earth was of importance for theologians since it ruled out, as geology had already done, the accepted Biblical chronology.

Let us now turn to a survey of such discoveries, and

[1] See further *Authority and Archaeology* (edited by Hogarth), 1899.

such use of neglected material, as were concerned directly with the Bible. Their real value is not, as the Fundamentalist vainly imagines, when they confirm statements in the Scriptures, but when they correct or supplement them.

For Old Testament studies,[1] in addition to the mass of material coming in from Babylon and Assyria, there may be mentioned the discovery of the Moabite Stone in 1868, of the Tell el Amarna tablets in 1887, as well as of numerous inscriptions in Arabia and North Syria. For the New Testament archaeology was not quite so fruitful, though mention may be made of J. T. Wood's excavations at Ephesus. The unearthing of the Egyptian papyri, however, showed that the Greek of both the Septuagint and of the New Testament was not unique, and inscriptions elsewhere demonstrated that it was by no means confined to Egypt. The discovery of the papyri followed the British occupation in 1882, but really systematic work did not begin until 1889. It was six years later that Grenfell and Hunt made their sensational discovery of words claimed to have been spoken by Jesus Himself, as well as a third-century MS. of Matthew i. The first to apply the new facts made available by the papyri was Adolf Deissmann in his *Bibelstudien* published in 1896. Work on the papyri aroused a new interest in Greek studies in general, and this was extended to Modern Greek, which W. F. Moulton had already used in his edition of Winer (*c.* 1870).[2]

New light also came from a keener study of Aramaic, presumably the original language spoken by Jesus and His disciples, and here the outstanding work was Dalman's *Die Worte Jesu*, published in 1898 and soon afterwards translated into English.

---

[1] See further Driver's *Schweich Lectures* for 1908.
[2] See further Thumb, *Greek in the Hellenistic Period* (1901).

E

Work on the text of the New Testament was also helped by the discovery of a new Syriac version of the Gospels by Mrs. Lewis at Mount Sinai. This was published in 1894.

Other discoveries which illuminated, if not the New Testament itself, yet the early days of Christianity, included *The Teaching of the Twelve Apostles* in 1883, the *Apology of Aristides* in 1891 and the Syriac and Latin versions of I Clement.

Of existing, but neglected, material, much now came to be used by theologians; the most important were the Jewish apocryphal writings. Up to the middle of the nineteenth century the only works that were at all well known were *The Testaments of the Twelve Patriarchs* and *IV Ezra*.

The growing historical sense found a further illustration in the greater desire to know more of the actual geographical background of the Bible. Palestine, it may be said, had been rediscovered by Edward Robinson in 1841. There followed a number of surveys as well as a spate of travel volumes. The Palestine Exploration Fund was established in June 1865, the corresponding German society not until 1877. Scientific excavation, however, had to wait until the arrival of Flinders Petrie from Egypt in 1890. The results to 1894 were summed up by George Adam Smith in his *Historical Geography of the Holy Land*.

The work of archaeologists and the narratives of travellers were also fruitful in another field, that of comparative religion, for they provided fresh material for the study of non-Christian faiths. This was really a new study, for though the early fathers, and even scholars in the thirteenth century, had noticed parallels between Christianity and other faiths, except in regard to Greek and Roman religion, and later to Islam, they had little available material, and in any case their work had been only superficial.

Much of the new material was due to Christian missionaries in different parts of the world and at work among very diverse peoples. Popular interest in the subject had been aroused in England by Carlyle's lecture on Mohammed in May 1840, delivered as part of his series *On Heroes and Hero Worship*. But now the study was attracting the attention of scholars. Much fresh information was supplied by E. B. Tylor in *Researches into the Early History of Mankind* (1865) and *Primitive Culture* (1871). For knowledge of more developed faiths men could turn to *The Sacred Books of the East*, a series edited by Max Müller. An attempt to arrive at some kind of a synthesis was made by Frazer in *The Golden Bough*, the first edition of which appeared in 1890.[1]

Jowett had foretold that no influence was 'likely to have greater power than our increasing knowledge of the religions of Mankind';[2] but for the anthropologist religion was merely one interest out of many, and he took little note of its spiritual significance. Religion might be merely something that mankind would outgrow as he became more rational, and ultimately discard; but the researches of anthropologists certainly produced evidence of the universal diffusion of religion, even if they gave no support to the traditional idea of a primitive world-wide revelation which had subsequently been lost.

The opinion that religion is but a passing phase in the life of mankind, might naturally suggest itself to those who studied the diverse and often contradictory forms which it had assumed among primitive peoples, for they

[1] Much fuller editions followed in 1907–15.

[2] *Epistles of St. Paul*, II, p. 186. F. S. Marvin, *The Century of Hope*, p. 220, considered that the tracing out of religious development was 'among the greatest of the conquests of the nineteenth century.'

had 'to become acquainted with so many grovelling and horrible superstitions that a presumption easily arises . . . that any belief which is religious is probably false.'[1] But such a view fails to take account of the ability which religions have shown gradually to purify themselves from unworthy and degrading elements. The idea of God, moreover, seems so deeply planted in the human soul that to eradicate it is not the easy task which some suppose, a circumstance which totalitarian states may one day discover to their cost.

The student of comparative religion must approach his subject without prejudice, assuming only that 'religion is a thing which has developed from the first, as law has, or as art has';[2] certainly he has no right to regard one religion as true, and the rest as false. This at once raises the question as to whether the Gospel is but one among many faiths, and whether a day will not come when it will be superseded by some higher faith in which all that is best in Christianity and in other religions will be combined. In any case how did it differ from its rivals, for it too preserved fables and fairy tales? One cause of Darwin's religious doubts was the realization that the Old Testament was 'no more to be trusted than the sacred books of the Hindoos.'[3]

Thus for the theologian a new outlook was necessary since it had to be admitted that religion had not been confined to a single line of development, going back to the Old Testament and the Jewish people. Moreover, the study of other religions helped to a fuller understanding of Christianity itself. This, however, did not mean that he could respond to appeals to take part in 'the common search after fuller truth and the higher life on equal

---

[1] W. James, *Varieties of Religious Experience*, p. 490.
[2] Menzies, *History of Religion*, p. 6.
[3] *Life of Charles Darwin*, I, p. 308.

terms.' Even if it was admitted that some knowledge of God could be acquired from other channels, those who believed that the supreme revelation was in Jesus could not but regard their faith as unique, and also as final. For them it was final because 'inseparable from the final victory which Christ accomplished.'[1]

None the less for the average Christian, to whom rumours of the effects of comparative religion had come, the situation was disquieting. For it seemed to be accepted not only that Judaism had much in common with other Semitic religions and had been influenced by them, but also that pagan elements had entered into the practice of the primitive Church and even into its doctrines. This unfolding of the genesis of his beliefs seemed an attempt to rob them of their sacred character. Others, more wisely, held that origin does not affect validity. But even such a standpoint has its drawbacks, for as Farnell has said: 'We can imagine how difficult it might be to maintain a fervid Mariolatry among sincere Christians, if the worshipper were vividly conscious that he was worshipping, not the historical personage, but another form of the great Pagan goddess of the Mediterranean.'[2]

Another difficulty was that experiences thought to be the privilege of Christians were also enjoyed by members of other faiths. The day had long passed when these could be explained away as the work of the devil intended to confuse the faithful. Such had been the belief of some of the early fathers, but Justin was wiser when he recognized that even before Christ there had been those who had had a genuine revelation of God.[3] This, too, is the teaching of the prologue of the fourth gospel which tells

[1] Quick, *Doctrines of the Creed*, p. 143.
[2] *The Attributes of God*, p. 8.
[3] *First Apology*, 46. Among the Greeks he specified Socrates and Heraclitus who 'lived according to reason.'

us that Christ is the light which lighteth every man (John
i. 9). Had some ultra-orthodox souls been better
acquainted with the Logos theology, they would have
been saved much needless heart-burning.

Attempts to bring home to the general public the true
meaning and value of comparative religion were scanty.
The matter was complex and not without its dangers to
the partially instructed. F. D. Maurice, as early as 1854,
had lectured on the subject at King's College, London;
but the first real consideration of the study, from a
Christian point of view, did not come until 1887 with
Boyd Carpenter's Bampton Lectures on *The Permanent
Elements in Religion*. The attempt was not without its
risks and in some minds at least the suspicion was aroused
that the lecturer himself was infected by a kind of lurk-
ing infidelity.

There was certainly a growing interest in the subject
among educated people though intellectual curiosity
rather than moral earnestness was, it is to be feared, the
prevailing motive. There was even some dabbling in
Oriental cults, though this was more common in America
than over here. For those who felt that they had ex-
hausted the possibilities of Christianity and were anxious
for some new thing they provided alternatives. Illingworth
tells of two women who were persuaded to attend a
missionary study circle and said afterwards: 'Brahminism
seems much more interesting than Christianity.'[1]

Before leaving the subject of comparative religion it
may be noted that in Germany the Ritschlians, in view of
their belief that only in Christ was there a revelation of
God, gave no encouragement to the study. When it was
proposed to establish a chair of comparative religion in
the theological faculty at Berlin, Harnack opposed the
scheme on the ground that other religions could make no

[1] *Life of J. R. Illingworth*, pp. 191 f.

contribution to theology, though they might be profit-
ably studied in connexion with history and philosophy.

Christianity is a historic religion, that is it bases its
claims on actual happenings in the past, and also includes
a long process of development. This last factor must not
be ignored; indeed Hort has said: 'The history of the
Church from its foundation to the present hour is hardly
less necessary to the Church at large than the Gospel
itself, whatever it may be to the individual disciple.'[1]
This being so it could not remain immune when new
methods were being applied on all hands.

Interest in the way in which Christianity had developed
had been aroused through the rise of the Oxford Movement with its appeal to history and the reaction it caused
in other schools of thought. Among Protestant theologians interest in the history of the Church was also
noteworthy, on other grounds, for they were coming to
value it, not so much as the guardian of tradition, but as
the continuous embodiment of the faith.

As was the case with science and philosophy, and,
indeed, in union with them, the impact of history with
its new methods and outlook was a cause of unsettlement.
For history was seen as the story of man's progress in
time and space, by which truth was gradually being
unveiled. This seemed to run counter to the idea of a
revelation given once and for all. Whilst it was recognized that Christianity had introduced fresh spiritual
forces into the world men must not allow themselves
to be too closely bound up with events which had taken
place in a distant past and in a simpler and less complex state of society. Here it may be noted that even
Gore admitted that there was a tendency 'to exaggerate
the extent to which the mere evidence of remote facts can
compel belief.'[2] Man must look forward and not back-

---

[1] *The Way, the Truth, the Life*, p. 35.   [2] In *Lux Mundi*, p. 247.

ward, and a vastly changed world demanded a fresh conception of spiritual things. Thus the view of history contained in the Bible, which may be called catastrophic, was to be replaced by a new conception of revelation as a continuous process; like creation itself it was still going on. This shifted the emphasis from revelation as the act of God, to revelation as the discovery of man. To some thinkers this seemed like a substitution of natural for revealed religion. But this is a false antithesis. All religion must have in it an element of revelation, for unless God willed it man could make no discoveries concerning Him. Here it may be observed that Clement of Alexandria had refused to make any distinction between what man discovers and God reveals;[1] and it is not out of place to compare Westcott's description of inspiration as partly the insight of holiness and partly its divine reward.

The Christian claim to a special revelation, however, depends ultimately on the way in which that claim is justified in the history of the world and of the Church; on whether, as H. F. Hamilton has written, 'when the scientific process is over, there are facts and considerations which make such an interpretation appear as part of a moral and intelligible system of progress.'[2] That such a revelation is continuous should present no difficulty to those who believe in the work of the Holy Spirit in the Church; provided always that there is no belittling of the unique revelation in the historic Christ. 'The gospel,' Gwatkin has said, 'is not a growth of this world, but a revelation from the unseen. Men do not set forth in it their passing opinions about God, but God reveals in Christ His own eternal thought.'[3]

We come now to a consideration of the application of

[1] See *Protrept.*, VI, *Strom*, I., v and xix.
[2] *The People of God*, I, p. xxxix.
[3] *The Sacrifice of Thanksgiving*, p. 10.

the new methods of historical criticism to the records of Christianity contained in the Bible. This was an urgent matter for the theologian, for so long as untenable theories of the inspiration and authority of the Bible prevailed there could be no bridging the gap between theology and the new knowledge. Biblical theology had to be built up on a solid foundation of ascertained facts; hence the true Fundamentalist is not he who refuses to allow any examination of the foundations of his faith, but he who strives to make those foundations as secure and sound as possible, even if the process requires the abandonment of cherished beliefs.

Before going further it may be well to recall that the Bible itself makes no claim to be 'history.' In spite of common usage the Old Testament had no 'historical' books, the Jews included Samuel and Kings among the Prophets; thus declaring that their purpose was religious, to tell of God's dealings with the race in the past. The same is also true of the gospels, for, though they are presented in a historical form, their primary function is to declare a message. Revelation in short was not given to satisfy man's intellectual curiosity but to instruct him concerning his relations with God and with his fellow man.

But if the Bible did not base its claims on being history, yet, like every other ancient record, it had perforce to submit to an intense scrutiny; so, indeed, alone could it preserve its influence and even its intellectual respectability. The scholars who undertook the task were inspired by no hostile spirit, on the contrary many of them were sincere believers; though Dr. Schechter accused much German criticism of the Old Testament as being a product of anti-Semitism.[1]

What it may be asked were the principles upon which Biblical criticism was based? In the first place, I would

---

[1] Quoted in *The People and the Book*, p. 406.

suggest, scholars endeavoured to discover what the records actually said, and what they meant to those who first heard or read them. This involved, secondly, the questioning of all allegorical and fanciful interpretations, such as had been traditional in earlier ages. The record must be permitted to speak for itself. But in listening to its voice allowance had to be made for the very different methods of thought and utterance customary at the time and in the place of its origin. Even to-day the mind of the Oriental works differently from that of the European, being careless of exact detail, and making statements which are not intended to be taken literally. So had it been with the Biblical writers and with those who later attempted to interpret them. The historical accuracy of the books, like their science, belongs to the age in which they were written.

In spite of many merits and much sincerity the work of critics in our period had its defects, some of them grave defects. As with other historians they were too much concerned with details, and the establishment of minute facts. Their whole approach was too analytical; they forgot that the Scriptures constituted 'a whole which had been felt as a whole by innumerable minds for many centuries.'[1] Also they were often blind to the underlying significance of the literature with which they were dealing. In some critics, more especially in Germany, there was a lack of reverence, of awareness that they were concerned with something sacred; they ignored the dictum of Bengel that before attempting to interpret the New Testament a man must ask himself if he had the right to do so. Hence many facile theories were advanced, and ready and rationalizing explanations sought for any seeming difficulties.

The chief credit for the advance in Biblical studies, and

[1] F. D. Maurice, *The Kingdom of Christ*, II, p. 145 (Everyman Edition).

in particular of New Testament studies, must be given to what is sometimes called the Cambridge school. This is generously admitted by Hastings Rashdall, an Oxford man, who says that they 'raised English theology . . . from a condition of intellectual nullity up to the level of the best German work, while they infused into it a character-istic English spirit of caution and sobriety.'[1] But to speak of a Cambridge school is perhaps a misnomer, for Cambridge, as Inge has said, 'has generally produced men rather than movements.'[2]

It was the theologians who first made use of the new historical methods in Cambridge, and in his inaugural lecture in 1884 Creighton turned to them rather than to the professed historians for examples of the way in which history should be studied.[3]

Theological studies in Cambridge during our period were dominated by three great figures: Lightfoot, who held professorships from 1861 to 1879, after having previously taught theology there; Westcott, who was Regius Professor from 1870 to 1890 when he succeeded Lightfoot—who had been his pupil—as Bishop of Durham; and Hort, who held professorships from 1878 to his death in 1892.

Lightfoot has been declared to be 'the greatest inter-preter of the New Testament in our day';[4] but in spite of his numerous and excellent commentaries he was a historian rather than a theologian. Speculation as such only interested him from the historical angle and he had no wide knowledge of philosophy, nor was he greatly concerned with doctrine, though he knew what had been

[1] *Principles and Precepts*, p. 164.

[2] *The Platonic Tradition in English Religious Thought*, p. 40.

[3] See *Historical Lectures and Addresses*, p. 2: 'The traditions of theological learning have been thoroughly leavened by the historical spirit. . . . Theology has become historical, and does not demand that history should become theological.'

[4] *Life of Bishop Percival*, p. 155.

written on the subject. His greatest achievement was the massive editions of some of *The Apostolic Fathers* which Cuthbert Turner considered to be 'the greatest contribution to patristic learning in the last two centuries.' The German Church historian, Harnack, was equally enthusiastic.

As a pure scholar Westcott was probably the least great of the three, and the long years he had spent in teaching at Harrow before his return to Cambridge had perhaps made his scholarship too classical. His work will scarcely endure as will that of Lightfoot, and he lacked the comprehensive learning and philosophical largeness of mind of Hort. In critical ability he was also a little deficient, being apt to be influenced by subjective considerations. But in his day Westcott exercised a much more widespread influence than the others. This was due to his interests outside scholarship, for he was deeply concerned over social problems and over the expansion of the Church in other lands. Westcott was primarily a religious teacher and guide, rather than an investigator of truth, and he saw the past largely in the light of the present and its needs; but by his emphasis on the teaching of the fourth gospel and his knowledge of the Greek fathers he helped to change the direction of theological thought in this country. He was the mystic and prophet of the little band, and though men might fail to understand many of his utterances they could not fail to be impressed by his spirituality and Christian zeal.

Hort's range of knowledge was more extensive than that of the other two; he was a competent student of natural science and had a philosophical mind. Hence he was more daring in speculation and less bound by orthodoxy. 'To identify [truth and orthodoxy],' he said, 'seems to me to involve the practical loss of either ... most orthodox criticism in England is reckless of truth and unjust to the authors of other criticism.'[1] He desired above all else to be a candid inquirer into the truth and even hesitated about accepting the Hulsean Lectureship because of 'a growing dislike of the position of a professed advocate.'[2] New truth, even if it appeared 'to be acting to the injury of faith,' was to be welcomed.[3] It would, however, be a grave mistake to imagine that he had doubts as to the truth of Christianity. When after his death the Hulsean Lectures were published under the title of *The Way, the Truth, the Life*, they demonstrated 'how openness of mind could coexist with an unshaken grasp of central truths,' and in them he presented a 'large and progressive faith which seemed as far removed from ordinary dogmatism as dogmatism itself from religion.'[4]

If Hort had not those practical gifts which enabled his colleagues to administer in succession the great diocese of Durham his devotion to scholarship was even greater than theirs. He regarded 'the steadfast and persistent pursuit of truth' as 'a moral and spiritual discipline,' involving 'a life of vanities abased and ambitions foresworn,'[5] Unfortunately he was handicapped by a temperament which disliked putting his thoughts into written form and by a shyness which interfered with personal intercourse.

Though the three friends worked together in continued co-operation there was no identity of outlook. Lightfoot and Westcott would nowadays, I suppose, be called Liberal Evangelicals, though the latter criticized the Evangelicalism of his day; but Hort was a convinced 'sacerdotalist.' Thus they produced no systematic theology, though it had been the ambition of Westcott

---

[1] Hort, *Life of F. J. A. Hort*, II, p. 147.
[2] *Op. cit.*, II, pp. 52f.   [3] *Op. cit.*, II, p. 156.
[4] *Op. cit.*, II., pp. 371 and 373.
[5] *The Way, the Truth, the Life*, pp. 93f.

to crown his own work by a treatise on Christian doctrine, for which he collected voluminous notes.

When Westcott resigned the Regius Professorship in 1890 he was, rather unexpectedly, succeeded by Dr. Swete. Although Swete, like Benaiah, the son of Jehoida, 'attained not to the *first* three' (2 Sam. xxiii. 23), he demands notice for the work which he accomplished during a perilous time of transition. By temperament he was fitted for this task, for though in his youthful days he had been a stern opponent of the new views, having said of Colenso: 'The axe raised by episcopal hands to fell the Pentateuch, is seen to be laid at the root of Christianity,'[1] by a gradual and almost unconscious process he had come to adopt a more critical position. Thus he was able to preserve Cambridge theology from indulging in dangerous ventures. He himself wrote largely and had a gift for organizing and encouraging the work of others. It was due to him that *The Journal of Theological Studies* was founded, as well as the Central Society for Sacred Study; and he did pioneer work in connexion with the text of the Septuagint of which he produced an edition (1887–94).

Much of the work of the Cambridge theologians took the form of exposition. Sanday, addressing a Cambridge audience, described it as 'the home of commentaries'[2]— and though this type of scholarship is often rendered obsolete with the growth of new methods and the discovery of fresh material, a great deal of it still has considerable value when the necessary modifications have been accomplished. This is, I think, because although apt to become a little over-absorbed in details of language and style they never lost sight of the real end of all

[1] *Henry Barclay Swete: A Remembrance*, p. 103. This volume contains an appreciation of Dr. Swete's contribution to theological learning from the pen of Dr. Bethune-Baker.

[2] *The Life of Christ in Recent Research*, p. 40.

theological study, or forgot that spiritual things are spiritually discerned. Lightfoot once remarked that the only way to know the Greek Testament properly is by prayer, and Scott Holland said of Westcott, 'He cannot venture to criticize a verse without a prayer.'[1]

Turning to the sister university we must first take note of the long and influential life of Benjamin Jowett, which ended in 1893. Jowett, in spite of much outward success, is a rather pathetic and lonely figure, for he was cramped by his peculiar temperament and limited outlook. He was, moreover, deeply disappointed by the effects of liberal views.[2] But he had a gift for discerning the significance of things and foretold many later developments. In one matter, however, he was unfortunate in his forecast for he doubted whether any considerable light would ever be thrown on the New Testament from inquiry into language.[3] But this was before 1860, and no one then imagined what was hidden in the sands of Egypt; so there was some excuse. As many regard Jowett as a kind of iconoclast it must not be forgotten that he had a profound feeling for the needs of ordinary Christians and was ever anxious to avoid offending Christ's little ones. If his theological learning was not very deep, and his knowledge of past work inadequate, he made a determined stand for freedom in research and interpretation, whilst insisting that theories should not outrun facts. Gore, who had been Jowett's pupil, always kept a portrait of him in his study. 'When I feel I am stressing an argument too far,' he once wrote, 'I look at Jowett and he pulls me up.'[4]

---

[1] *Life of H. S. Scott Holland*, p. 59.
[2] At the end of his life when trying to persuade Cosmo Gordon Lang to undertake theological teaching at Balliol he confessed, 'We don't seem able now to inspire the young men. *We may have truth . . . but we have no fire.*' J. G. Lockhart, *Cosmo Gordon Lang*, p. 101.
[3] *Essays and Reviews*, p. 477. [4] *Life*, pp. 38 f.

The outstanding figure in Oxford theology during the closing years of our period was William Sanday, who first became a professor in 1883. With a wide knowledge of the work of German and American scholars he was perhaps less informed of what was being done in France. Although cautious by nature, he gradually advanced; at one time, for example, he accepted the truth of miracles which he would later deny. One of his great merits, as with Swete at Cambridge, was the encouragement of younger men whom he gathered round him in seminars, a method not very common in England at that time.

But the most important contribution to theology made by Oxford in our period came from the *Lux Mundi* group, of which Gore was the leader. As a boy at Harrow he had been inspired by Westcott, though this influence affected his practical work, such as social reform, rather than his theology, and, as we have just seen, he had been trained by Jowett, and so was ever suspicious of mere conjectures. He aimed above all at definite results, even if these were incomplete.

The importance of *Lux Mundi* lay not so much in its contents as in the manner of its origin. It was the production of a body of earnest thinkers, possessed of a common outlook to an extent greater than that of most who co-operate in such enterprises, thinkers who had long been striving to reconcile the claims of reason and of revelation. They held a strongly dogmatic faith and were completely loyal to the Creeds, hence their object was to demonstrate that the new knowledge which had come to their generation was capable of being combined with everything that was essential in orthodox Christianity. They had no desire to expound new truths, but so to interpret traditional ideas that they might be understood by their contemporaries.

When *Lux Mundi* appeared in 1889 it met with a very varied reception. To the older generation, of whom Liddon was typical, it came as a grievous shock and surprise; though Liddon himself ought to have been less surprised than others for he had written to Scott Holland in 1884: 'I have feared sometimes that the younger Churchmanship of Oxford was undergoing a silent but very serious change through its eagerness to meet modern difficulties and its facile adoption of new intellectual methods, without fully considering the uses to which they might be put by others.'[1] The outcry, however, was nothing like so vehement as that which had greeted *Essays and Reviews* thirty years earlier; but even so there were those who demanded that the contributors should resign their orders. The latter, it may be remarked, were equally surprised at the outbreak. Scott Holland wrote: 'We seemed to ourselves to have been saying these things for years; and to have heard everybody else saying them. Now suddenly we find it all spoken of as a bomb.'[2] They were naturally distressed at the pain caused to men to whom they owed so much, but held to their position, and the outcry soon passed. Many of them went on to occupy high positions in the Church and university.

If the older Anglo-Catholics were alarmed by *Lux Mundi* to liberal theologians it was a disappointment. 'It has a more friendly and Christian tone,' wrote Jowett, 'than High Church theology used to have, but it is the same old haze and maze—no nearer approach of religion whether to morality or to historical truth.'[3]

In spite, however, of this and similar criticisms *Lux Mundi* undoubtedly did much to spread moderately liberal views among Churchmen, especially among those of the Anglo-Catholic school, and to give them counten-

---

[1] *Life of H. Scott Holland*, p. 112.
[2] *Op. cit.*, p. 281.   [3] *Life*, II, p. 377.

ance and a certain respectability. It also helped many of
the younger generation to whom the Christianity of
Liddon was 'impossible to believe,' and that of Jowett
'not worth believing,'[1] to consider once again the claims
of the historic faith; and that was no small achievement.

[1] Cf. *Life of Charles Gore*, p. 119.

Lecture Four

BIBLICAL THEOLOGY

THE growing interest in Biblical studies during our period is reflected in the immense production of literature dealing with the subject. Smith's *Dictionary of the Bible* had begun to appear in 1859, but the end of the century saw more adequate publications of this nature. The first volume of Hastings' *Dictionary of the Bible* came out in 1898, to be completed six years later. It represents a somewhat cautious and conservative point of view. The same cannot be said of its contemporary, *The Encyclopaedia Biblica*, published from 1899 to 1903. The Old Testament articles were many of them marred by the eccentricities of Cheyne, who was one of the editors, and those on the New by the drastic criticism of certain continental scholars. These theories have been decisively rejected by later writers.

Each of the two older universities began a series of special studies; the *Studia Biblica* of Oxford in 1885, and the more ambitious Cambridge *Texts and Studies* six years later. Special periodicals were also being produced such as *The Expositor*, *The Expository Times*, and in 1899 *The Journal of Theological Studies*. Biblical scholars could no longer be content with the space allocated to them in classical and other journals.

The most striking evidence for renewed interest in the Bible, however, is to be found in the numerous series of commentaries which began to be poured forth. One of the earliest of them was suggested by the Speaker, and to it Westcott contributed the volume on St. John which appeared in 1880. Dr. Pusey had projected a series of commentaries to uphold traditional views, in which he hoped that Liddon would co-operate. But nothing came of it save his own *Minor Prophets* (1860–77) which, though showing great learning and spiritual insight, is quite devoid of critical judgment.

Dr. Smith had intended to supplement his *Dictionary of the Bible* by a series of commentaries, but the project was dropped in 1863. Macmillans had already approached Westcott, who was to have taken part in Smith's proposed series, and eventually he, with Lightfoot, Hort, and Benson, agreed to write on the various books of the Greek Testament.[1] Westcott was to be responsible for the Johannine literature, including Revelation; Lightfoot for the Pauline epistles; Hort the Synoptic gospels, Acts, and the remaining catholic epistles. In the end Benson produced Revelation, Westcott his portion, and also Hebrews, Lightfoot most of the Pauline epistles, but Hort failed completely with his share, and it was only after his death that incomplete, but exceedingly valuable, comments on part of James and of I Peter appeared, and also Rev. i–iii. From Cambridge there came also the well-known Cambridge Greek Testament, and the Cambridge Bible for Schools and Colleges.

A very popular series was the *Expositor's Bible* which, as its title suggests, was homiletic rather than critical. It included four outstanding volumes by G. A. Smith, two on Isaiah (1888–90) and two on the Twelve Prophets (1896–98). *The Expositor* was also responsible for a commentary on the Greek New Testament in four volumes. Towards the end of our period the International Critical Commentary began to appear with a very high standard of scholarship. Two notable volumes

[1] See *Life of Hort*, I, pp. 371f., 417f., *Life of Westcott*, I, pp. 205ff.

from British scholars were published in 1895: Driver's Deuteronomy and Romans by Sanday and Headlam.

For Introductions to the Bible English scholars for long relied on those published in Germany and France, some of which were translated. Then came Driver's *Introduction to the Literature of the Old Testament* to which nothing quite comparable on the New appeared in our period, though Samuel Davidson was used, and there was also, from across the channel, Salmon's valuable work.

Concordances were also beginning to appear. Hatch and Redpath to the Septuagint, and Moulton and Geden to the New Testament, both in 1897. Thayer-Grimm's lexicon of the New Testament came out in 1888, but students of Hebrew had still to be content with a translation of Gesenius, though already a new lexicon, based on Gesenius, the well-known Brown, Driver, and Briggs, was in hand. The first part appeared in 1891, but it was not completed until 1906.

Turning to a more detailed examination of the work done we begin naturally with the Old Testament. As long ago as 1830 Milman's *History of the Jews* had aroused some concern, for he treated the Jews as an Oriental people and described Abraham as a 'sheikh'; but it was not until 1862 when the first of Bishop Colenso's studies on *The Pentateuch and Joshua* appeared that alarm became acute. Colenso was a mathematician, and he was worried by the numerous inconsistencies which he found in the figures of the Pentateuch. He confessed that he could accept a miracle, but not a false arithmetical statement. His writings had no positive value, but they served to draw attention to obvious difficulties and the need for fuller inquiry. In 1862 also Stanley published the first volume of his *History of the Jewish Church*. His position was much that of Ewald whose *History of Israel* he translated (1869–80). Ewald, by later standards, was conservative in his views, but they held their ground until the more radical and consistent position associated with Graf and Wellhausen became known. Wellhausen published his *Prolegomena to the History of Israel* in 1878, but it was not translated until seven years later. In the meantime the new standpoint had been expounded by Robertson Smith in articles in *The Encyclopaedia Britannica* and in his lectures on *The Old Testament in the Jewish Church*, published in 1881. The persecution he had to face in his native Scotland drew public attention to the whole subject.

The name of Robertson Smith will always be associated with the attempt to place the religion of the Old Testament in the setting of Semitic religion in general. He himself paid a well-deserved tribute to the work of Dr. John Spencer, Master of Corpus Christi College, Cambridge, who in the latter half of the seventeenth century had laid the foundations of the study in his *Ritual Laws of the Hebrews* written in Latin. Although the writings of Robertson Smith seem to show that Old Testament religion was the outcome of a process similar to that undergone by other Semitic religions, he always refused to accept such a conclusion.[1] He was justified inasmuch as though religion among the Jews may have had the same origins, it rose to spiritual heights far beyond the reach of the rest.[2]

When Dr. Pusey's long tenure of the Regius Professorship of Hebrew at Oxford was ended by his death in 1882 he was succeeded by S. R. Driver, to whom Old Testament studies in England owe so much. Driver had

[1] See Black and Chrystal, *Life of W. Robertson Smith*, pp. 536 f.

[2] Cf. Driver, *Schweich Lectures*, p. 90: 'Archaeology demonstrates . . . that though the religion of Israel was built upon the same material foundations . . . it rose immeasurably above them; it assumed . . . a unique character, and in the hands of its inspired teachers became the expression of great spiritual realities such as has been without parallel in any other nation of the earth.'

just become convinced of the truth of the Graf-Wellhausen theories and did much to commend them. His *Introduction to the Literature of the Old Testament* which appeared in 1891 is a landmark, showing the extent to which modern views were being accepted in England.[1]

The chief contentions of the new criticism were that the Law in its present form was later than the Prophets. The writings of the latter were accepted as units (with some additions and insertions) save in the case of Isaiah, where xl–lv and lvi–lxvi were held to be later, and Zech. ix–xiv.

The Pentateuch was divided up between a number of sources, some ancient, some post-exilic; and attempts were made to trace out in minute detail the various documents.

The Psalms were brought down to a late date, though it was not denied that older material was contained in them. Not only were they deprived of their Davidic authorship, but the various historical settings were also rejected. For many this robbed them of much interest; but it may be pointed out that their spiritual value was in no way impaired, indeed it may be argued that this was deepened by the divorce from supposed temporal and local circumstances.

Of the other books in the Writings, as the Jews called the third division of their canon, the Wisdom literature was ranked as exilic or post-exilic, Daniel was placed in the Maccabean age, whilst Chronicles was seen to be a late rewriting of the older books in the age of Ezra-Nehemiah.

These results were regarded as 'assured,' and though they have been challenged in recent years, and many

[1] See also S. A. Cook, 'The Present State of Old Testament Research,' in *Cambridge Biblical Essays*, pp. 53 ff.

diverse hypotheses offered in their place, they may, I think, still be said to stand in broad outline.[1] But even in the nineteenth century there was by no means full agreement amongst critics as to many points, a circumstance of which their opponents made full use to discredit the entire critical movement.

Many of these opponents had no right to express any opinion on the subject, at least from the point of view of scholarship, and their main weapons were abuse and ridicule. They waxed facetious over Pentateuchal criticism, pointing out that though the Mosaic authorship was denied, the Pentateuch itself had been reduced to a 'mosaic.' They forgot that a work may be a 'mosaic' and yet have its own pattern, and that wise borrowing is often a sign of true genius. Others, whose learning cannot be denied, also took up the challenge. Pusey produced a large volume in 1865 in defence of the traditional date of Daniel, and less qualified scholars also wrote in support of the traditional views. Their works brought assurance to the unlearned, who often did not realize the large concessions which were made to the critical position, even when it was rejected as a whole. This applies to Hommel's *Ancient Hebrew Tradition*, translated in 1897, and the various writings of that eccentric archaeologist, Professor Sayce, including *The Higher Criticism and the Monuments* published in 1893.[2]

Some of the theories put forward by scholars, and above all by Cheyne, were so extreme and fanciful that they excited derision even more than alarm, and undoubtedly hampered the spread of more reasonable views. But the work of sober scholars, and above all of Driver, gradually made its way, and conciliated opposition;

[1] See further H. H. Rowley, *The Growth of the Old Testament* (1950).
[2] Orr, *The Problem of the Old Testament*, though it did not appear until 1905, represents the conclusions of the best conservative scholars. It, too, makes a number of concessions.

though even Driver's *Introduction* called forth a protest which was signed by many of the clergy.

We come now to the New Testament and here the general tendency, towards the end of our period, was in a conservative direction, especially in the case of Acts and the authorship of the Pauline epistles. Dr. Lock in his inaugural lecture as Dean Ireland's Professor in 1896 pointed out that classical writings—he gave Aristotle's *Poetics* as an instance—are accepted as genuine on evidence which is much more slender than that demanded for New Testament writings.[1]

The chief interest of New Testament scholars was a desire to know more of the life of Jesus and of His teaching. The amount of literature produced directly on this subject was enormous and has been well summarized in Schweitzer's well-known volume, the English translation of which bears the very appropriate title, *The Quest of the Historical Jesus*. Two works, however, may be mentioned owing to their wide popularity, Renan's *Life of Jesus*, which was translated soon after its appearance in 1863, and *Ecce Homo*, published anonymously in 1865 and later acknowledged as the work of Seeley, the Cambridge historian. Though Seeley's volume was thought by many to be an attack on orthodox Christianity, this was not the author's intention. He wished to study Jesus as a man

In the last few years of our period a new conception of Jesus began to arise by which He was regarded solely as a prophet proclaiming the speedy end of all things, 'the ecstatic herald of the Kingdom of God.' This eschatological interpretation came as a reaction from the predominant Liberal Protestant view in Germany which looked upon Him as little more than a teacher of morals and the example of a perfect life. Such a concep-

[1] Printed in *The Bible and Christian Life*, p. 70.

tion, it was felt, failed to account fully for Jesus and for the effects of His ministry. The new view certainly brought out some neglected aspects of the New Testament picture, but as is so often the case with German scholars it was pressed too far. Its advocates did not face the possibility that the two strands might be combined. In England it was welcomed by those who considered that the divine immanence had been over-emphasized, as well as the importance of the picture of Jesus in the fourth gospel, where eschatology is allowed only a subordinate place.[1]

The publication of editions of Jewish and early Christian apocalyptical writings had already aroused a fresh interest in the subject and provided material for its study. Unfortunately Schweitzer, the chief exponent of eschatological views, had little first-hand knowledge of this literature, as Charles, in the preface to the second edition of *Eschatology* published in 1913, pointed out. Dalman had already protested against fanciful pictures of Jewish messianic hopes in the time of our Lord.[2]

Turning to the gospels themselves we find that two great problems faced scholars: (a) the origins and mutual relations of the first three gospels, generally known as the Synoptists; and (b) the authorship of the fourth gospel and its relation to the other three. It might seem that too much attention was paid to these problems to the neglect of the contents. There was certainly a danger that they might be regarded as, in Burkitt's words, 'the beginning and end of serious Gospel study, rather than as questions that must be settled because on other grounds we have to study the Gospels.'[3]

[1] The popular idea that eschatology is absent from the fourth gospel needs considerable modification: see Howard, *Christianity according to St. John*, pp. 106 ff.
[2] *The Words of Jesus*, pp. 132, 248.
[3] In *Cambridge Biblical Essays*, pp. 195 f.

The numerous likenesses between the first three gospels had in older days been readily explained as due, not to any kind of dependence upon one another, but to their common inspiration. But this did not explain their diversities. In our period there were three suggested lines of explanation: (a) dependence on a common oral tradition, a theory held by Westcott and popular in England, though not of much account elsewhere; (b) direct borrowings from each other; and (c) the use of common sources. The Tübingen school in Germany had accepted Matthew as the oldest of the gospels,[1] but it soon came to be seen that this would not work, and a general consensus of opinion gave Mark the priority, holding that he had been used by Matthew and Luke.[2] Some scholars even suggested that there was an Ur-Marcus lying behind Mark, so as to account for cases where Matthew and Luke agree against him. Another factor demanding explanation was the presence in both Matthew and Luke of passages, mainly of teaching, which are not found in Mark. To account for them another source, called Q, was suggested, since it seemed unlikely that there had been borrowing between Matthew and Luke. Attempts to reconstruct this supposed document have been made, but none of them is satisfactory, for it may be taken as certain, in view of their use of Mark, that not all of it appears in either Matthew or Luke.

By the end of the century there was considerable agreement on the problem. It was accepted that Mark was the earliest gospel and that he, and at least one other source, had been used by the other two. But much was still left unexplained, such as the exact nature and

[1] It represented Ebionite views for them, whilst Luke was Pauline, and Mark an attempt at reconciliation.

[2] As late as 1884, however, E. A. Abbott, *The Common Tradition of the Synoptic Gospels*, rejected the use of Mark by the other two.

contents of Q, and the origin of matter peculiar to Matthew and to Luke. There was also uncertainty as to the dates of the various gospels. Behind all this a more fundamental problem was still unsolved. That is, how far the gospels give an entirely reliable picture of the earthly life and teaching of Jesus, in view of possible doctrinal modifications by the early Church. Such modifications can be seen already at work in the way in which Matthew and Luke made use of Mark. Did they also antedate Mark himself? Thus there was a tendency to a kind of stalemate, for behind Mark and Q there seemed to be a whole period of which nothing definite was known.

In the matter of the several gospels there was also in England a fair amount of agreement. The traditional authorship of Mark was accepted and also the probability of Petrine influence. Rome was favoured as the place of writing and a date between 65 and 70. The so-called little apocalypse (ch. xiii) was held by many to be a separate document and there was difference of opinion as to the original ending of the gospel.

The authorship of Matthew, and its place of origin, were felt to be insoluble problems. The date also was uncertain. It was obviously later than Mark, and might be later even than Luke.

Since nearly all English scholars agreed that Acts came from the same pen as Luke questions concerning this gospel could not be considered in isolation from it. There was a tendency to put it rather late in view of a possible dependence on Josephus. As both may have used a common source this is by no means necessary. The statement in Luke i. 1 that many had already produced gospels was also taken, quite needlessly, as a sign of late date. But it was generally agreed that it was written after the Fall of Jerusalem in 70 A.D.[1]

[1] See further Armitage Robinson, *The Study of the Gospels* (1902).

We come now to problems connected with the fourth gospel. The question of authorship remained, as it does to-day, a debatable matter. The traditional authorship was strongly supported by Westcott, Hort, and others; but the difficulty that there is no evidence that the apostle was ever at Ephesus, the generally accepted place of the gospel's origin, was not met. There was equal difficulty over the supposed 'John the Elder.' Taking the gospel as it stands it was regarded as an attempt to readjust the Christian message to a new age and new conditions, with perhaps a too great emphasis on its Hellenistic character. At the same time some of the historical allusions were accepted as preserving a genuine tradition and even as correcting statements in the Synoptists. That the author knew the latter was often assumed. In Germany Wellhausen and E. Schwartz had suggested that behind the gospel there was an original document which had been worked over by a later hand; but this idea received little favour in England where the tendency was to regard it as representing the meditations of St. John in old age. But even if this were true the question remains as to what were facts and what were the fruit of the apostle's own pious imagining.[1]

The vindication of the early date and genuineness of the Acts was a striking feature of our period. The Tübingen school had seen in it a late document put out to conciliate the various warring elements which they had discovered in the primitive Church, and in Germany many still clung obstinately, as Harnack observed as late as 1906,[2] to some such hypothesis. Those who accepted the authenticity of the work received a welcome and unexpected reinforcement from Sir William Ramsay, the

[1] See further Howard, *The Fourth Gospel in Recent Criticism and Interpretation*, Sanday, *The Criticism of the Fourth Gospel*, and Edwyn Hoskyns, *The Fourth Gospel*, pp. 17ff.
[2] *Luke the Physician*, p. 7.

archaeologist and classical scholar, who, having approached the Acts as a forgery of the mid-second century, was compelled to change his view by the knowledge which the author evidently possessed of places mentioned by him in Asia Minor. At first Ramsay accepted this only for the 'we passages,' but later he came to the conclusion that the whole was by St. Luke. His two volumes, *The Church in the Roman Empire* (1893) and *St. Paul the Traveller* (1895), made an impressive contribution to the subject.

There are really two problems connected with the authorship of Acts; the relation of the so-called 'we passages' to the rest of the book, and the connexion with the third gospel. Renan, it may be remarked, had accepted the Lucan authorship before 1883. As early as 1892[1] Harnack became convinced that the 'we passages' were by the same author as the rest of the book, and, though not so decidedly, that that author was St. Luke; but it was not until after our period that his well-known works on the subject were written. In England a vigorous plea for the early date of Acts was made by R. B. Rackham in the first volume of *The Journal of Theological Studies* (1899), which he followed up by his well-known commentary in the Westminster series.[2]

As in the case of Acts there was a decided move in a conservative direction in the criticism of the Pauline epistles. Baur had accepted four only, but the opinion that nine at least were genuine was gradually prevailing,[3] and many scholars, I think quite rightly, added Ephesians. The Pastorals were more doubtful, though some who rejected them were prepared to admit that they contained Pauline material.

---

[1] *Texte und Untersuch*, VIII, iv, pp. 37ff.

[2] See further J. W. Hunkin, the late Bishop of Truro, in Jackson and Lake, *The Beginnings of Christianity*, II, pp. 396ff.

[3] The Dutch scholar Van Manen rejected all of them; but found few to agree with him.

There was certainly a growing interest in the Pauline writings as providing reliable material for a period about which there was much uncertainty. In some this took the exaggerated form of claiming that St. Paul was the real founder of Christianity as it developed in the second generation. The relation of St. Paul and Jesus was, however, not much studied in England and America, though it received great attention in Germany and only less in France. It was also being recognized that his letters having been written to meet special occasions were not well suited to form the basis of any dogmatic system.

The most important contribution of English scholarship came from Lightfoot. His commentary on Galatians appeared in 1865 and set a new standard for such productions. Philippians followed three years later and Colossians in 1875. Some notes on other epistles were published in 1895 after his death. English scholars were pretty well agreed in their views of the Pauline epistles, save in the case of Galatians, where Ramsay had revived the so-called South Galatian theory which had originally been put out in 1867, but without attracting much notice. By this theory the recipients of the letter were not some otherwise unknown Christians in the north of the province, but those whose evangelization is recorded in the first missionary journey in Acts. The acceptance of the theory involved for some scholars a much earlier date for Galatians, making it the first of all the Pauline epistles.[1]

Of the remaining books of the New Testament not much need be said. Westcott brought out a commentary on Hebrews in 1889. It had originally been arranged that Hort should undertake this volume, and had he been able to do so his commentary would doubtless have been very different from that of Westcott, whose knowledge of the Old Testament and of Judaism in the Christian era was

[1] See further Schweitzer, *St. Paul and His Interpreters.*

not so profound. Westcott also published a commentary on the Johannine epistles in 1883. Over the other Catholic epistles there was some uncertainty. Most English scholars, led by Mayor, held James to have been written by the brother of the Lord, though on the Continent it was generally given a late date, perhaps the middle of the second century. Much the same opinions were held in regard to 1 Peter. As to 2 Peter and Jude, with which it is closely linked, there was a tendency to regard them as late documents, though some accepted Jude as genuine.

On the book of Revelation there was no striking contribution by English scholars, for though Benson's commentary appeared in 1900 it lacked any sufficient knowledge of the Jewish background. Hort had lectured on the first three chapters in 1889 and his notes were published in 1908. Hort placed the book under Nero, rejecting the prevailing idea that it was written under Domitian, and Sanday, in his preface to Hort's posthumous volume, was inclined to take the suggestion seriously, though he recognized its difficulties, as, indeed, Hort himself had done. It made easier the attribution of both Revelation and the gospel to St. John, since the differences in style and ideas might then be accounted for by lapse of time. The Tübingen school had accepted Revelation as by St. John, but had rejected the gospel. Conservative scholars in England were inclined to accept both, but the more advanced suggested that they were the product of a single group in Asia Minor, though by different authors.

Having thus very cursorily dealt with the historical criticism of the New Testament we come now to consider its textual criticism.[1] In the case of a collection of documents such as the New Testament, where the

[1] See further Kenyon, *The Textual Criticism of the New Testament* (1901).

interpretation of a passage may depend on a single word, it is obviously of the utmost importance that a correct text should be established. The received text, which underlies the Authorized Version, came from an age when the principles of the science were but little understood, and, moreover it is based on inferior MSS. Attempts to arrive at a better text had already been undertaken before 1860 by Lachmann, Tregelles, and Tischendorf, but no very serious changes had been contemplated. However, after Tischendorf discovered Codex Sinaiticus in 1859, he published a much more radical text. Still further changes followed the release of Codex Vaticanus some ten years later.

It is, however, to the English scholars Westcott and Hort, and above all to the latter, that the great advance in textual criticism is due. If they made no discoveries of new MSS. the materials collected by others were used to the full. Their text did not appear until 1881, and in the introduction Hort laid down the principles which must underlie all adequate textual criticism. The theory of Westcott and Hort, which depended on the division of the MSS. into families, was not entirely novel, for it went back to Griesbach, but they applied it in a new way. The MSS. were arranged in four groups. The Received text, which they called the Syrian, was placed later than the rest; and the greatest reliance was placed on the Neutral group depending on the two great codices, Vaticanus and Sinaiticus. Related to this was a group known as the Alexandrian, and, finally, there was the Western text which had been widely current in the second century and was to be found mainly in Codex Bezae, the Old Latin, and other versions.

When the text was published it had to meet fierce criticism. Dean Burgon, the principal defender of the Received text, was no mean scholar and controversialist.

G

He ridiculed the notion that the true text had been lost for fifteen hundred years and that it was to be found only in two MSS. He also drew attention to some weak points in the theories underlying the text which would later be developed. But less prejudiced scholars gave the new text their commendation; some even felt that the last word had been said on the subject. This, however, was too optimistic; for fresh discoveries and later work suggest that the Western text, regarded by Westcott and Hort as a corruption of the Neutral, deserves much more consideration. But such criticisms as have arisen affect but a few passages, and in Westcott and Hort, or something very like it, we have a more solid foundation for the text of the New Testament than exists for any other ancient writing.

The realization that the Received text was unreliable led the Canterbury Convocation in 1870 to appoint a committee, on which scholars who were not Anglicans were invited to serve, to revise the Authorized Version. The New Testament appeared in 1881, the same year as Westcott and Hort's text, and was followed by the Old Testament in 1885, and the Apocrypha ten years later. The Revised Version, however, was not too well received. It was certainly more exact than the Authorized,[1] but it was unfamiliar, and had lost literary grace. Many of the changes were small and unimportant, and seemed unnecessary. There is no doubt that the version suffered from having too many 'cooks,' and in any case the attempt was premature. Armitage Robinson has said: 'It is one of the tragedies of Scholarship that the version was made a generation too soon.'[2]

The text of Westcott and Hort was perhaps the greatest

---

[1] In some passages the A. V. is definitely misleading: e.g. when following the Vulgate it speaks of men *being converted*, whereas the original Greek is active (cf. Matt. xiii. 15, Mark iv. 12, Luke xxii. 32, Acts iii. 19, xxviii. 27).

[2] In *Lightfoot of Durham*, p. 126.

single contribution to biblical studies made by English scholars in our period, but there was much else of which we may well be proud. If it was not on so vast and comprehensive a scale as that of the Germans, it represented much solid work, though in the light of further progress it now seems a trifle timid and overcautious. But the fact that it was less spectacular and experimental was really an advantage; for a slow growth is not subject to those reactions which so often follow more revolutionary changes.

In addition to work on the Old and New Testaments which has already been noticed there was much admirable work on early Church history, where Lightfoot's *Apostolic Fathers* was outstanding. These researches also threw fresh light on the background of the New Testament with part of which some of them were probably contemporary. Much attention was also given to patristic commentators and a number of new editions were produced, such as Swete's *Theodore of Mopsuestia on St. Paul* (1880) and Brooke's *Origen on St. John* (1896).

As a consequence of all these labours on the Bible a number of points gradually became clear, at least to thinking men. It was recognized, for example, that the Bible was not all of a piece, but the outcome of a long development. Even the New Testament was seen to possess different layers, for ideas and doctrines are found in the Pauline epistles and in the fourth gospel which are absent from the earlier records of the Synoptists. In the past both orthodox and sceptics had regarded the Bible as a single whole; now they could agree that its contents were diverse, and that a more discriminating approach was necessary.

Other points which may be mentioned are the discounting of allegorical interpretation, as a result of which many passages in the Old Testament regarded as Messianic forecasts had to be rejected. Again, the comparative study of languages had demonstrated that the languages in which the Bible had been written were not unique. Hebrew was merely one member of a group, and not, as some had supposed, the language used in the Heavenly courts; whilst the Greek of the Septuagint and the New Testament was found to be merely that used in the contemporary world.

The attempt to treat the Bible like any other book,[1] and to apply to its contents the methods of historical criticism probably caused more unsettlement than any other factor. Quite apart from its supposed results the very attempt seemed to savour of blasphemy; and though conservatives might scoff at the variety and contradictory nature of many of the new theories, none the less they had a kind of cumulative effect and aroused much alarm. This was increased by the fact that critical inquiries were only possible for the few, and that no distinction was made by traditionalists between the reverent scholarship of those who sincerely held the Christian faith and the wildest of rationalists. Indeed the use of such methods and the acceptance of such views by some of the clergy, and their prevalence in the universities, was a most potent cause of irritation and distress.[2] If once you begin to tamper with the Bible where will you stop? So it was asked; and even Carlyle, in spite of his real admiration for Dean Stanley, once remarked, 'There's that Dean, down in the hold; bore, bore, boring, and some day he will bore through and let all the water in.'

[1] The Bible, of course, cannot be treated exactly as any other book, for it is wrapped up in the history of the society which produced it—the People of God. Moreover its very subject-matter makes it different from any other collection.

[2] Cf. Davidson, *Life of A. C. Tait*, I, p. 276.: 'The science of reverent Biblical criticism was, to most people, absolutely unknown . . . and it is difficult to realize the vague terror with which much of what is to-day the general belief of Christian men was lumped together as "Rationalism".'

Criticism of any and every kind seemed a direct challenge to the traditional view of the inspiration of the Bible, a view which was held by Evangelicals and Tractarians alike. But the traditional view rested on very insecure foundations, and had no justification from the Bible itself, though this was often cited. In reality it was based on an erroneous interpretation of the phrase 'the word of God,' and had been taken over from the Jewish view of the Old Testament and then extended to cover the New. It is to be remembered that the Church has never defined what the inspiration of the Bible exactly is. At the time of the Reformation stress had been laid on the witness of the Scriptures and exaggerated ideas as to the meaning of their inspiration had gradually imposed themselves on later Protestant thought. Luther himself was rather an iconoclast, for not only did he reject James as 'an epistle of straw,' but also Revelation, and found more of a gospel in St. Paul's epistles than in the Synoptists. He also laughed at the childishness of Jonah and denied the Mosaic authorship of parts of the Pentateuch.

The popular view of inspiration depended on a complete ignorance of the way in which the canonical books had been selected by the Church, and men talked as if the Bible in its present form had dropped from Heaven. Englishmen in practice believed in the inspiration of the Authorized Version, and there is a story of a mythical workingman who gave up Christianity when assured that the Bible was not written originally in English.

The moral difficulties of the Old Testament were ignored or explained by allegory; but such evasion was no longer possible when the Bible was treated like other literature. It may be noticed that the early fathers had regarded much in the Old Testament as wrong in itself, but as suited to the training of the Jewish people, a view with which modern critics would hardly quarrel.

The idea of an inspired book is difficult to conceive, unless, indeed, the writers were mere scribes who wrote from dictation. This was the prevalent view, under the form of what was known as verbal inspiration—hence the alarm over textual criticism. A deeper knowledge of the ways of God with man would have exposed the unworthiness of such a conception. Divine providence had decided that our Lord should leave behind Him no written words. Had such been sanctioned they might have prevented further investigation of the truth, except by allegorical methods. The theory of verbal inspiration seeks 'to do what our Lord was careful not to do . . . to put our Gospels in the position that actual writings of our Lord would have held.'[1] Furthermore a verbally inspired book cannot be translated—the position of Islam which regards any attempt to translate the Quran as sacrilege. The Jews got over this difficulty by the legend that the seventy translators of the Septuagint each produced an identical rendering, and thus demonstrated that they were equally inspired with the original writers.

A more worthy conception of inspiration places it, not in the separate writings, but in the Bible as a whole. It also regards the writers, rather than the writings, as inspired. By this means the freedom of the individual is preserved and his special gifts allowed expression. 'Inspiration is surely not incompatible with considerate workmanship,' A. C. Bradley has written of the poet,[2] and the same is true of the writers of the canonical books.[3]

Those who held that every single word in the Scriptures was inspired were naturally not content with

[1] Latham, *Pastor Pastorum*, p. 15.
[2] *Shakespearean Tragedy*, p. 68.
[3] See further Sanday's Bampton Lectures for 1893.

obvious interpretations, they also sought for 'hidden meanings'; hence the cult of 'prophecy,' a cult which provided so useful an occupation for retired army officers in our inland watering places, though the invention of cross-word puzzles may have made it less popular. No one, of course, would deny that new light is ever breaking from the Bible, for as George Herbert has said, 'Thy word is all if we could spell,'[1] but methods of interpretation must be controlled by reason and worthy of their subject.

Older methods of interpretation had made a great use of isolated texts and, indeed, treated the Bible as if it were a legal code, or a formal treatise. Modern methods take a different line and study the general development of thought and institutions, endeavouring to discover exactly what each writer meant by what he wrote. Furthermore the idea that the Bible is the best commentary on itself has to be modified. Since the authors came from an immense variety of times and circumstances they held views which were often contradictory or at least hard to reconcile. Even in the New Testament terms were used in different senses by different writers.

If the first effect of the application of the new methods was to arouse alarm and disquiet in the minds of many believers, especially among simpler folk, its results were not entirely negative. Further reflection showed that they might be the means of teaching fresh lessons and of quickening insight into divine truth. As such they were welcomed by many serious and devout Christians. The hand of God might after all be seen in what had been thought of as a sheer deprivation. It is thus that God ever trains His children. 'If He takes away any familiar signs of His presence, it is because they are becoming hindrances to the ripening of discipleship.'[2] Even the moral

[1] In *The Flower*.   [2] Hort, *The Way, the Truth, the Life*, p. 34.

limitations of the Old Testament and its crude ideas of the Almighty were no longer a difficulty. 'To the modern mind the Bible would be incomplete . . . if it did not include the traces of childhood's faith as well as the matured experience of the perfect man.'[1]

But the new teaching undoubtedly made it more difficult for the average Christian to read and understand the Bible; since study and effort were demanded, which many either could not or would not supply. Hence perhaps the decay of the habit. Even the 'Helps' which were soon provided were not of much value, as they paid too much attention to small points of detail, such as might be useful for examination purposes, but gave little assistance in bringing out the spiritual message.

For many scholars and educated people the authority of the Bible is greater than ever as a result of the intense critical examination to which it has been subjected. If it is not so absolute neither is it so vulnerable, because more rational. But for the common people the case was far different. To them the Bible, taken literally, had been the bedrock of their religion. Englishmen are a forthright and truth-loving race, and disinclined to make fine distinctions; so it was a case of all or nothing. If some things in the Bible were untrue, could anything be accepted? Who were they to decide on any particular statement when scholars themselves were not in entire agreement? So there followed a reaction from the narrow and even superstitious views of inspiration and infallibility which they had too readily received. The consequences were something of a catastrophe, for the Bible came to be neglected, and even its higher truths and noblest teaching were robbed of authority. I wonder if something of this growing distrust lies behind the story of the small girl who, during the South African

[1] Allen, *The Continuity of Christian Thought*, p. 393.

War, on being told by her mother about Jonah and the whale asked if it were true. Her mother replied: 'Of course it's true, it's in the Bible.' 'Yes, Mummy—but has it been confirmed by the War Office?'

Lecture Five

DOGMATIC THEOLOGY

THE mind of man, in so far as he thinks at all, is naturally curious, and sooner or later it demands that his beliefs should find an intellectual expression. At first those who were capable of making such a demand were but few, hence the divorce in the ancient world between philosophy and religion. Religion was then the concern of the state or community, and was limited to the performance of certain ritual acts. So long as men took their part in such acts, they were free to interpret them as they thought fit. It was otherwise in the Christian Church and from early days attempts were made to formulate its fundamental beliefs.

Such a process can never be entirely successful for it seeks to express in human words and forms eternal truths which ever elude them. None the less some definite pattern of belief was necessary, for dogma not only crystallizes experience, it should also promote it; hence the futility of a merely barren orthodoxy. The bare intellectual acceptance of a creed has no spiritual value, and is, as Dr. Lock has said, 'like the answer to a sum which a schoolboy takes from a key.'[1] But since dogma depends on experience the process of defining it can never be complete.[2] The development of doctrine, moreover, is no unbroken advance, it involves readjustment, and even the abandonment of outmoded forms of expression.

[1] *The Bible and Christian Life*, p. 244.
[2] Cf. Westcott, *Lessons from Work*, p. 13. 'as long as experience is incomplete there can be no finality in the definition of doctrine.'

'Progress in theology,' Hort has said, 'does not consist in mutilation, but in purification. It is not the great facts or ideas that are false, but the way they are conceived.'[1]

The early fathers of the Church had not been at all anxious to define the dogmas of the faith too narrowly or exactly. Not only did they recognize the impossibility of finding adequate language, but they were also conscious that sufficient knowledge was unattainable. Athanasius himself has said, 'God has His being beyond human discovery' (*Contra Gentes*, II), and, in the less speculative West, St. Hilary of Poitiers is very outspoken in the matter. It was the false teaching of heretics which had compelled the Church to dare 'to embody in human terms truths which ought to be hidden in the silent veneration of the heart.' He even ventured to admit that in so doing the Church had dealt with 'unlawful matters and trespassed on forbidden ground,' and that attempts to define the divine nature were 'helpful to man rather than descriptive of God.'[2] Such admissions of man's limited knowledge and the early reluctance to add to the number of doctrinal statements should be borne in mind in approaching the study of dogmatic theology in the nineteenth century.[3]

Unfortunately later Christian thought largely followed other lines, and during the Middle Ages a desire to leave nothing unexplained led to the over-elaboration of definition.[4] Dean Colet condemned this as due to 'temerity and pride,' and it undoubtedly led to what Gore has called 'a passionate desire to get back to the

---

[1] *The Way, the Truth, the Life*, p. 186.

[2] See *De Trin.*, I, 19;, II, 2 etc., and on the reluctance to define, Illingworth, *The Doctrine of the Trinity*, ch. vi.

[3] Cf. Archbishop Lang's opinion: 'I . . . have always . . . regarded any attempts, however authoritative, to formulate beliefs in God as necessarily only "symbols".' J. G. Lockhart, *Cosmo Gordon Lang*, p. 13.

[4] It was not, however, considered unorthodox to distinguish between the essential nature of God and the forms by which we perceive it.

Christ of the Gospels and of the primitive Church.'[1]
Erasmus, in the preface to his *Enchiridion*, written at Basle
in July 1518, pleaded that statements about the faith
should be as few and as simple as possible. But his
warning remained unheeded.

In the Roman Church the itch to add to the dogmas
of the faith has persisted. Perhaps in order to make a
'hedge about the Law,' and so to protect more vital
beliefs; perhaps also to demonstrate that she still possesses
the necessary inspiration. Such fencing of the truth by
supplementary barriers seems very far from the methods
of Jesus, and such additions are apt to strain the allegiance
of the sincere and thoughtful, and to turn away those
who would enter. Florence Nightingale told Cardinal
Manning that though her heart was urging her to find a
long-desired refuge in the Church of Rome, her head
refused to assent to Roman doctrines—and so she
remained in the Church of England.

Christian belief as it came down to the later nineteenth
century was full of discords and apparent contradictions.
This was the result of attempts to combine and comprehend diverse strands of tradition, dating back to the
struggle, in the earliest days, between the Hebraic and the
Hellenistic elements. Now the influx of new knowledge
made for further discords and difficulties.

According to the sixth of the Thirty-nine Articles of
the Church of England the creeds are based on the Scriptures. If this is so, then the results of Biblical criticism
demanded a re-examination of all doctrines to bring them
into line with more adequate methods of interpretation;
for as F. H. Chase has said: 'The History of Doctrine cannot rightly be understood apart from the History of
Interpretation.'[2]

---

[1] *Dissertations*, p. 181.
[2] *Chrysostom: A Study in the History of Biblical Interpretation*, p. viii.

Difficulties in connexion with dogmatic statements brought about by the changing climate of thought, however, seldom cause anxiety to the average church-goer, even if he realizes them. By long usage he has got into the habit of taking so much for granted. He has, for example, been told that the *seventh* day is to be kept holy, when everybody knows that it is the *first* that is meant. But to the outsider, even if he is being drawn to Christianity, such contradictions are a real obstacle; he is amazed that they are allowed to persist, and gains the impression that there is a different standard of intellectual integrity within the Church from that expected amongst scholars.

Hence there arose among thoughtful Churchmen a demand, which grew in intensity during the last quarter of the century, for some kind of restatement of doctrine, and for the elimination of expressions of belief which were no longer adequate.[1] So conservative a scholar as Dr. Swete felt that such demands ought to receive sympathetic consideration, for, as he wrote, 'The disciples of the Word dare not turn away from any of the teachings of God in Nature and History because they may be thought to involve reconstruction of some of their cherished beliefs.'[2]

But it was not only on intellectual grounds that there was criticism of the Church's dogmas, some of them revolted the growing moral sense of mankind. This was so especially in regard to certain theories of the Atonement and the belief in eternal punishment. Both had been attacked by Bishop Colenso in his commentary on Romans in 1861. This raised an outcry at the time as coming from a bishop, but it was soon lost in the still greater excitement over his criticisms of the Pentateuch.

[1] It may not be out of place to point out that science is equally guilty in retaining expressions which have lost their meaning. It can speak of splitting the atom, which is sheer nonsense, for an atom is that which cannot be split.

[2] In *Cambridge Theological Essays*, p. ix.

The so-called Athanasian Creed was also a serious stumbling-block. A writer of wide influence wrote to Archbishop Tait: 'I believe that this Creed has done more to alienate the minds of intellectual men from the Church of England than all other causes.'[1]

There was, however, in many quarters a reluctance to undertake the task of restatement. For those who rejected Biblical criticism it was uncalled for. Others had so great a veneration for the traditional definitions that they felt that such attempts were almost blasphemy and a questioning of the guidance of the Holy Spirit in the past. It is as easy to give undue weight to ecclesiastical pronouncements as to other authoritative utterances and to

> Deem our puny boundaries are things
> That we perceive and not that we have made.

They were also afraid of making any concessions in view of efforts to explain Christianity in terms of comparative religion, and especially did they dislike the emphasis laid on similarities, real or supposed, between certain Christian doctrines and ideas found in other religions. This latter difficulty was met by A. L. Moore who affirmed that 'A truth revealed by God is never a truth out of relation with previous thought. He leads men to feel their moral and intellectual needs before He satisfies either.'[2]

One reason why the strictly orthodox regarded any tampering with even a single doctrine as perilous, was the traditional idea that all doctrines were, so to speak, interlocked, and that to abandon or restate one might jeopardize the whole structure. Even A. L. Moore could say: 'It seems to me impossible to defend Christianity on anything less than the whole of the Church's Creed.'[3]

[1] Davidson, *Life of A. C. Tait*, II, p. 129.
[2] In *Lux Mundi*, p. 66.
[3] *Science and the Faith*, p. xii.

A more worthy attitude surely was that of F. H. Chase who affirmed that 'The thoughtful Christian . . . will be content to admit that round his central beliefs there lies a margin of admittedly open questions. The cry "all or nothing" is the confession of despair'.[1] At the same time it must be conceded that many quite legitimate attempts at restatement were vitiated by a lack of a sense of proportion.

Between the older and younger adherents of the Oxford Movement there was in this matter, as in others, a notable difference. This can be seen by a comparison of two statements. Liddon had affirmed that 'A particular intellectual presentation of Truth may be modified, but nothing of the kind is possible with any article of the Christian Faith.'[2] But Illingworth could write: 'Christian truth, in virtue of its very vitality . . . must be for ever outgrowing the clothes with which successive ages invest it.'[3]

Before proceeding to examine various doctrines in detail it will be well to notice a feature in the general theological development of our period which affected many of them—a fresh turning to Greek theology. A knowledge of Greek theology had been characteristic of the Caroline divines; hence, in the judgment of Hort, their largeness of mind.[4] But Greek theology had fallen out of favour, and the Tractarians, in particular, had paid undue deference to the more rigid theology of the Latins.[5] A reaction was undoubtedly overdue, and in the preface to *Logic and Life* (1882), Scott Holland in emphatic terms drew attention to the loss which English theology had sustained through its neglect of the Greek fathers.

---

[1] In *Cambridge Theological Essays*, p. 417.
[2] *Life*, p. 366.   [3] *Life*, p. 45.   [4] *Life*, II, p. 38.
[5] The leaders had, of course, read the Greek fathers, Newman especially delighted in them (R. D. Middleton, *Newman at Oxford*, p. 107), but the movement was little affected by them.

The revival of interest in Greek theology was due in part to the influence of F. D. Maurice. Essentially a theologian, all his practical teaching was based on theology, and on a theology which in its turn was not the outcome of thought and meditation alone, but had been hammered out in real life. His influence would undoubtedly have been much greater had it not been hampered by obscurities of style, and even of thought. Men suspected him, as he himself confessed in April 1862, of hiding some esoteric doctrine behind utterances which were intended to be taken quite literally. In 1873, the year after Maurice's death, Matthew Arnold wrote: 'The truth must at last be said, that in theology he passed his life beating the bush . . . and never starting the hare.'[1] None the less he exercised a profound influence on some of the younger men, such as Hort, though strangely enough Westcott who held very similar views owed nothing to him.[2] In our own day there has been a praiseworthy return to the study of his ideas and teaching.[3]

Turning to the different articles of belief we begin naturally with the idea of God; for this is fundamental to all theological thinking; fundamental, moreover, for conduct as well, since our conception of the moral law must vary with our idea of God. Ethics for the Christian cannot be divorced from metaphysics.

The predominant feature of our period, following on the revived interest in Greek theology, was a new emphasis on the immanence of God who was thought of more and more, not as standing outside the world, but as continually active in human affairs and in nature. This new emphasis was also in agreement with the discoveries

[1] *Literature and Dogma*, p. 345.
[2] See *Religion in the Victorian Era*, pp. 296f.
[3] E.g. A. R. Vidler, *The Theology of F. D. Maurice*, and A. M. Ramsey, *F. D. Maurice*.

of natural science, for when heaven was looked upon as a place above the earth it was easy to think of God as dwelling there. The abandonment of such a conception materially altered the situation. Moreover natural science seemed also to reveal God continually at work in the natural creation. The move away from the old idea of God as almost purely transcendent, which was really an inheritance from Deism, was necessary, and, on the whole, beneficial, for as Tennyson wrote in 1869, 'The general English idea of God is as of an immeasurable clergyman: and some mistake the devil for God.'[1] But too great an emphasis on the divine immanence had also its dangers, for it might take away from the uniqueness of the Incarnation, and undoubtedly verged on Pantheism. The Higher Pantheism, as it was called, was, indeed, proving very attractive in our period to some who had a romantic and poetic outlook. It was a kind of cosmic emotion, but unlike the older Pantheism strove to preserve human personality and freedom.

The Christian idea of God as Love aroused various problems for believers, and evoked denials from non-believers. The age was becoming increasingly humanitarian and even sentimental, and was also tending to identify evil, not as the Christian does with sin, but with pain and suffering. Thus the presence of pain in the world seemed inconsistent with the benevolence or the power of the Creator. On this question Illingworth made a noble contribution.

The Christian doctrine of the Trinity was a real difficulty to many, mainly owing to the use of 'person' to describe the Father, Son, and Holy Spirit. The belief of the average Christian was, in fact, Tritheism, a belief in three gods. Rashdall, at the price of being suspected of unorthodoxy, met the difficulty by drawing attention

[1] *Memoir*, II, p. 90.

H

to the teaching of the older theologians that the three 'persons' are not 'distinct centres of consciousness,' but 'eternally distinct activities of One Divine Mind.'

Rashdall also did good service, and with the same risk, by his teaching on the Incarnation, in which he laid stress on the perfect manhood of our Lord. This was virtually ignored in popular belief which regarded Jesus as 'not really man at all, but simply God walking about with a human body.'[1]

For philosophy the Incarnation raises many difficult problems which largely remain insoluble, for they concern the relation of a concrete human life to a divine universal. Theologians, too, were engrossed in our period with the relation of the Jesus of history and the Christ of dogma. The problem had become urgent following Hegel's attempt to bridge the gap between the divine and the human. It need hardly be said that it was in Germany that most of the work was done, but English theologians took their part and that in a more conservative spirit. One of the most striking utterances was contained in Harnack's famous lectures at Berlin in the winter of 1899–1900, under the title of *Das Wesen des Christentums*, soon translated into English as *What is Christianity?* Harnack professed to believe in the divinity of Christ, but was impatient of orthodox methods of explaining it.

The traditional theology of the Church had treated the relation of the divine and the human in our Lord as primarily a question of metaphysics. For medieval theologians, as for the popular conception of Christianity in the nineteenth century, the divinity was all-important, the manhood little more than a mask. But now the problem was being approached from a different angle in consequence of the new interest in history and psycho-

[1] *Principles and Precepts*, p. 41.

logy. There was an attempt to solve it by the so-called Kenotic theory, based on the statement in Phil. ii. 7 that Christ 'emptied himself.' It sought thus to account for the limitations of our Lord's knowledge, a fact which is recognized in the Synoptic gospels which speak of His growth in knowledge and also of His ignorance in certain matters (Mark xiii. 32, Luke ii. 52; cf. John xi. 34). This theory had long been known on the Continent through the work of Thomasius (d. 1875) and Godet (d. 1900). In England attention to it was drawn by Gore in *Lux Mundi* and in his *Dissertations* published in 1895.

The sub-title of *Lux Mundi* had been 'A Series of Studies in the Religion of the Incarnation' and this reflected a change of emphasis in English theology. The prevailing Protestantism had made much of the Atonement as the central doctrine of Christianity. That this should have been so is easy to understand, for the consciousness of the work of Christ in the individual soul was to many so vivid that it constituted for them the most certain proof of Christianity itself. They regarded the Crucifixion as the divine remedy for the fall of man and the sole hope of the race.

But the renewed study of the Greek fathers, and especially of the Alexandrians, showed that there were other ways of viewing the matter. They held that the Incarnation was no mere afterthought, made necessary by man's failure, but had been part of the divine plan from the beginning, and was, indeed, the natural sequel to the creation of man. Man had been made in the divine image and the Logos, or Word of God, had ever been at work in the world preparing the way for the supreme revelation of Himself in a historical person. Thus the Incarnation, as the crown of a long process, and not as a remedy for a catastrophe, could itself be regarded as the Atonement, the bringing together of God and man.

The death of Jesus must not be separated from the life which had gone before it. That life, whatever else it did, had taught men 'that in the conditions of the highest human life we have access, as nowhere else, to the inmost nature of the Divine.'[1]

Apart, however, from this emphasis on the Incarnation at its expense, there were other factors at work to lessen the importance of the Atonement in Christian thought and life. There was, indeed, almost a revolt, not so much against the doctrine itself, as against the crude theories which had been put forward to explain it; for the Atonement accepted joyfully in the simple language of the New Testament may become repellent when couched in the terms of scientific theology; and, 'circumscribed by the presuppositions of self-interest,' it is, as Oman has said, 'reduced to a selfish and immoral trust.'[2]

There is no 'official' explanation of the Atonement, and Gregory of Nazianzus could say that the death of Christ is an article of faith about which it was not dangerous to be mistaken; but certain views had become traditional. These may be divided up into three groups. (1) The theory held by St. Anselm, the Reformers, and prominent in Evangelical teaching, by which Christ suffered in the place of sinners, and so made expiation to God. In our period R. W. Dale published *The Atonement* (1875) which gives classic expression to this view. But already there were demands for a moralizing of the theory and for an abandonment of a merely individual reference in favour of one more social. These views found written expression soon after our period in the works of P. T. Forsyth,[3] who insisted that the reconciliation made by the Cross was 'a reconciliation of the world

---

[1] Pringle-Pattison, *The Idea of God in Recent Philosophy*, p. 157.
[2] *Vision and Authority*, p. 240.
[3] See especially *The Work of Christ* (1910).

as a cosmic whole.'[1] (2) The Representative theory
going back to the Greek fathers by which Christ as man's
representative performs an act of vicarious penitence.
This view was set out by M'Leod Campbell in *The
Nature of the Atonement* (1856) who stated that 'While
Christ suffered for our sins as an atoning sacrifice, what
He suffered was not . . . a punishment.'[2] (3) Finally the
theory associated with the name of Abailard,[3] by which
the effect of the Atonement was regarded as subjective,
an appeal to man to respond to God's love by the
example and inspiration of Christ's sacrifice. This view
was set out later by Hastings Rashdall in his Bampton
Lectures for 1915 on *The Idea of Atonement in Christian
Theology*.[4]

Criticisms of current theories of the Atonement,
especially of those which involved substitution or
representation, caused some alarm, above all in Evangelical circles. They had, however, a beneficial side, since
the traditional views tended to narrow religion by
making it too individual and even selfish, and by creating
a barrier between the secular and the religious, thus
excluding whole areas of human activity from the sphere
of religion. It was one of the merits of the *Lux Mundi*
group that they reminded men that the great theologians
of the past had regarded redemption as a means to an end,
'the reconsecration of the whole universe to God.'[5]

Other criticisms of the doctrine came from outside the
Church, by which the very possibility of any atonement
for sin was rejected. The law of consequences must work
itself out. This was a central point in the teaching of

---

[1] *Op. cit.*, p. 77.   [2] *Op. cit.*, p. 101.
[3] The word is one of four syllables; the common form Abelard, derived
from the French, is therefore incorrect.
[4] See further J. K. Mozley, *The Doctrine of the Atonement*, pp. 173ff., and the
collected volume of essays, *The Atonement in Modern Religion* (1900).
[5] *Lux Mundi*, p. 134.

George Eliot, who 'thought that the world would be infinitely better and happier if men could be made to feel that there is no escape from the inexorable law that we reap what we have sown.'[1]

One further reason why the doctrine of the Atonement began to fall into the background was that men were no longer worrying about their sins, and many, accepting views based on evolution, regarded evil as a thing from which man would gradually free himself, thus treating a moral as though it were a physical defect. According to these thinkers, who emphasized man's dignity and denied his depravity, evil consisted in the inability of man to realize his true nature. The thought of sin, that is disobedience to a divine law, was completely ignored.

We turn now to a subject which aroused considerable controversy and discussion, that of miracles. As knowledge of nature was extended into ever fresh fields anything like a violation of her laws became more and more repugnant to contemporary ideas. Long before, indeed, Pope had described a God who would interfere with the course of nature as being like 'some weak prince . . . prone for his favourites to reverse his laws.'[2] Those scientists who were critical of orthodox religion regarded any kind of miracle as an unworthy piece of magic, forgetting that 'behind a miracle there is an intelligible purpose.' It must be confessed that some apologists for Christianity had given them excuse for such an attitude, for there had been an appeal to miracles as, with prophecy, among the strongest of the 'proofs' of the Gospel. This appeal, however, had not been so extensive as is often supposed. The Alexandrian fathers had attached little value to the evidence of either miracles or prophecy, and Luther had said that 'external miracles are the apples

---

[1] Lord Acton, *Historical Essays and Studies*, p. 284.
[2] *Essay on Man*, IV, 121f.

and nuts which God gave to the childish world as play-things; we no longer have need of them.'[1]

Historical criticism naturally regarded all stories of miracles as of doubtful value and ascribed them to un-trained observation or unverified inference. One fact emerged which caused some concern, that was that the evidence outside the Christian tradition was as strong as that for even the miracles of the Bible.[2] In England the tendency was to reject many of the miracles of the Old Testament but to be chary of touching those of the New. There was, however, a complete change of point of view; miracles instead of being used as evidence for the truth of Christianity were now to be accepted because of Chris-tianity. They were, moreover, no longer looked upon as violations of law, but as made necessary by the sin of mankind which had thrown the world into disorder. Those theologians who were acquainted with natural science rejected any idea of arbitrary interferences; such actions would be, as Aubrey Moore told the Reading Church Congress in 1883, 'as fatal to theology as to science.'[3] The renewed emphasis on the immanence of God, however, helped theologians to find evidence for the divine providence not in supernatural interferences, such as might befit a transcendent deity, but in the constant ordering of nature.[4]

The growth of scientific knowledge brought up the question of the possibility of man's survival of the death of the body, and also, if this were not ruled out, the nature of any future life. Attempts to prove survival

[1] Quoted by Allen, *The Continuity of Christian Thought*, p. 286.

[2] Cf. Streeter, *Restatement and Reunion*, p. xii: 'It is . . . less the weakness of the evidence for the Biblical miracles than the strength of the evidence for others, that constitutes the main difficulty at the present time.'

[3] *Science and the Faith*, p. 225.

[4] Cf. Quick, *The Doctrines of the Creed*, p. 40: 'It is a false supernaturalism which would teach that God's activity in the created world is to be looked for mainly in occasional acts which are to be conceived of as interventions from without into its ordered working.'

were undertaken by the more learned along the lines of what is known as psychic research, by others, through recourse to spiritualism, though the two were apt to be confused. As to the future life itself it was seen that since heaven could no longer be regarded as a place the descriptive imagery of the Bible was not to be taken literally.

Those who rejected man's immortality tried to find compensations for the loss. The Positivists made for themselves an object of worship by combining what was noble and good in the lives of the great men and women of the past, and so claimed to give them some kind of immortality. Comte himself had said, 'the dead do not cease to live and even to think in us and by us.'[1] This was a poor sort of immortality, but it is significant of the interest taken in those who were gone.

Among theologians there was much speculation as to the nature and meaning of the resurrection body. The popular idea was, and I suppose still is, that the very material of our bodies will be reassembled. But a more worthy doctrine involves nothing more than the preservation of personality. Crude and materialistic views, in spite of St. Paul's warning that the new body would be a spiritual body (1 Cor. xv. 44), had prevailed in the early Church, but thinkers of that age made no clear distinction between mind and matter and so can be excused for mistaken ideas; but these have persisted and even find a justification in the fourth of the Thirty-nine Articles. The insistence on the resurrection of the 'body' was doubtless intended to demonstrate that the Christian doctrine was not, as with the Greeks, mere immortality. Lightfoot has laid down two valuable principles concerning this matter: (1) As far as we know the union of the soul of man with an external framework is essential;

[1] *The Catechism of Positive Religion*, p. 73.

and (2) We must not suppose that the resurrection body is like our present body.[1]

These questions, although they aroused much interest, did not provoke any violent controversy. This cannot be said of another aspect of the future life, the punishment of the wicked.

The controversy had begun before our period when in 1853 F. D. Maurice had affirmed that 'eternal punishment' did not mean something which went on for ever with no hope of repentance on the part of the sinner. It broke out afresh in 1878 when Canon Farrar, as he then was, proclaimed the doctrine of what he called 'Eternal Hope.' Here it may be noted that Westcott stated that it was 'just what he had himself been teaching for the last ten years.'[2] But orthodox theologians could not accept it. Liddon, although he admitted that the idea of men being tortured for endless ages was 'unspeakably awful,' yet concluded, 'it is revealed; and there is nothing more to be said.'[3] This argument, however, was rejected by more liberal theologians; not only was it repugnant to their moral sense, but in view of passages which suggest a very different conception, they also challenged the assumption that it was the only doctrine revealed in the Bible.

Criticism of the doctrine of endless punishment undoubtedly robbed the preacher of a potent weapon, and also had no small part in encouraging lax views about sin. Like so many reactions it was carried too far, and men, forgetting Christ's own warnings as to future retribution, came to look upon God as too good-natured to inflict any punishment at all.

The Oxford Movement had brought the question of the Church prominently before men's minds, and all

---

[1] *Notes on the Epistles of St. Paul*, p. 215.
[2] Quoted Rashdall, *Principles and Precepts*, p. 169.
[3] *Life*, p. 225.

through our period it was a subject which aroused great interest and revealed very diverse views. Some New Testament scholars rejected the idea that Jesus Himself ever intended to found such a body—typical of this opinion is Hatch as he expounded it in his Bampton Lectures for 1880 on *The Organization of the Early Christian Churches.* It was strengthened towards the close of the century by the eschatological school which regarded Jesus as convinced that He would quickly return. Statements in the gospels, and above all in St. John, were explained away as due to the natural tendency of the early Church to bolster up its authority. For such scholars the real founder of the Church was St. Paul. Such arguments, however, carried little weight with Anglican theologians, even when they did not go all the way with the Tractarians and their followers. Lightfoot and Westcott, not to mention Hort, were strict in their churchmanship, and their attitude caused some distress and bewilderment among Nonconformists, especially as Lightfoot's famous essay on *The Christian Ministry* was taken in a sense which he himself did not admit. Meanwhile the followers of the Oxford Movement were developing a view of the apostolic succession which was almost purely materialistic.[1]

The renewed emphasis on the idea of the Church was on the whole a healthy thing, for it helped to counteract the excessive regard for the individual which was characteristic of Evangelical teaching in the Church of England and among Nonconformitsts. The Church it came to be seen was no merely voluntary collection of believers, but a living and organic body; an idea which slowly sank in, and has been welcomed, since our period, in some rather unexpected quarters. It was certainly in line with the growing realization of community life in general.

[1] See my *Beginnings of Western Christendom,* pp. 319f.

In spite of all this, however, the authority of the Church, especially so far as the Anglican communion is concerned, declined seriously in the closing years of the nineteenth century. The extreme form in which it was stated by some Anglo-Catholics provoked a reaction, for it savoured too much of Popery. The English have always been anti-clerical and afraid of ecclesiastical domination. What, however, did more to undermine the prestige of the Church of England than any other cause was the refusal of individual members to submit to its rulings. This was especially true in the controversy over ritual which attracted wide and even violent public attention. There was much talk of clerical lawbreakers, and the defiance of the bishops, the constitutional instrument by which the Church expressed its mind and administered its affairs, aroused much unfavourable comment. If the Church could not exert authority over its own members it was obviously in no position to retain influence with those outside, or even their respect.

As to the Church in general there had grown up the not unjustified suspicion that there was one standard of truth for the scientist, and another for the ecclesiastic. The traditionalists helped to confirm this suspicion by refusing to make any concessions to modern ideas. Liddon, indeed, felt that in *Lux Mundi* there had been an abandonment of ground won by the Oxford Movement and a willingness to substitute private judgment and literary criticism for the authority of the Church.[1]

Turning to the subject of the sacraments we can only notice the development of eucharistic theology, a subject which had been much neglected since the seventeenth century. Here again there was an effort to redress the balance, and to view the subject less solely from the individual standpoint. People were reminded that the

[1] *Life*, p. 371.

eucharist has a God-ward as well as a man-ward aspect, and that it not only provides food for the soul, but is an offering to God by the whole Church of Christ in accordance with His own ordinance.[1] As regards the individual there was also development in the increasing emphasis on Christ's presence in the elements, an emphasis which aroused much controversy in the Church. The holding of what are now called round-table conferences[2] did little to assuage it.

For many devout Churchmen religion without dogma seemed meaningless,[3] and even those who could scarcely merit the term saw its importance. Did not Disraeli once say to Dean Stanley, 'Mr. Dean, no dogmas, no deans'?[4] But the tendency of the age was moving in an opposite direction, and so strongly that the future of dogmatic religion seemed to be hazardous. As early as 1863 Newman had written from the Oratory at Birmingham that he despaired 'about the cause of dogmatic truth in England.'[5]

The reasons for this were many and various. I think that one contributory cause was the feeling among some quite orthodox believers that the process of definition had gone too far, that the piling up of dogmas had obscured the simple Gospel. There was also a suspicion, that theologians were too much interested in minute points which did not really matter, and that they professed to have knowledge of things which were really beyond human attainment. Such a suspicion had considerable

[1] Cf. F. Paget in *Lux Mundi*, p. 308 (quoting W. Shirley, *The Church in the Apostolic Age*, p. 103): 'It is the strength and glory of Christian doctrine that it essentially "leads on to something higher—to the sacramental participation in the atoning sacrifice of Christ."' Liddon regarded Paget's essay as a real contribution to Christian theology (*Life*, p. 367).

[2] The round table was once the symbol of romantic and ideal endeavours, as now of more prosaic, if not less fruitful, enterprises.

[3] Cf. Newman, *Apologia*, p. 54: 'I cannot enter into the idea of any other sort of religion; religion as a mere sentiment, is to me a dream and a mockery.'

[4] *Memoir of Alfred, Lord Tennyson*, II, p. 232.

[5] *Autobiography of Isaac Williams*, p. 131.

justification as attempts to explain the mysteries of the faith, from the Atonement to the sacramental presence, were far from convincing, and depended largely on outworn philosophical notions. The terms in which some dogmas were stated had become mere words from which the reality they had once embodied had long departed. The effort of theologians to preserve the old forms, whilst giving them new meaning, may have been sincere and indeed praiseworthy, but it was not calculated to increase their credit with the masses.

In view of the prevailing uncertainty extreme liberals wished to establish 'an intellectual position for the Christian faith which should not be called in question by every advance in historical evidence and in physical science.'[1] This attempt to hold dogmas apart from history and science naturally brought discredit on dogma as a whole, and even so open-minded a theologian as Hort denounced it as 'a baseless contrivance for generating results of conduct such as would please God and make man happy.'[2] Others, including T. H. Green,[3] regarded dogma as a thing of the past. 'We must,' said William James, 'bid a definite good-bye to dogmatic theology. In all sincerity our faith must do without this warrant.'[4] A similar conclusion had been reached, rather plaintively, long before by Matthew Arnold in *Dover Beach* and *Obermann Once More*:

> Alone, self-poised, henceforward man
> Must labour; must resign
> His all too human creeds, and scan
> Simply the way divine.

[1] Arnold Toynbee's introduction to T. H. Green, *Two Sermons*.
[2] *The Way, the Truth, the Life*, p. 45.
[3] See *Memoir*, p. 147, where he says of dogmatic theology that it is 'a phase of the human mind in which, having lost its hold on the original religious experiences of the founders of Christianity, it substitutes for them chains of reasoning the same in kind as those by which it would explain or establish any physical or historical phenomenon.'   [4] *Varieties of Religious Experience*, p. 448.

For many earnest seekers after truth dogmas were a positive handicap, fettering the free movement of thought. Truth in their view could only be attained by the healthy conflict of ideas, and in this endeavour those whose intellects were already bound by ecclesiastical formulas could take no useful part.

In the decay of dogmatic religion many consoled themselves with the thought, so suited to a humanitarian and philanthropic age, that what really mattered was to live a Christian life, to follow the teaching and example of Jesus, not to hold any special opinions about His person. Conduct was the vital test, not the acceptance of credal statements. Such a conclusion sought justification in the attitude of Jesus Himself, as portrayed in the Synoptic gospels. A writer in *Essays and Reviews* had already contrasted His severe condemnation of the moral failings of the Pharisees with His apparent unconcern over the doctrinal defects of their rivals. Others quite openly rejoiced at what they regarded as the collapse of dogmatic religion. 'The worship of deities has passed into the service of man,' wrote Cotter Morison in the volume of that name. But such was not the universal opinion of those who could no longer accept the dogmas of the Christian faith. Their removal seemed only to add to the prevailing confusion. 'The absence of definite dogmas,' wrote John Addington Symonds in 1882, 'accentuates our present differences and makes the isolation of souls more painful.'[1]

In so far as they emphasized the practical nature of religion, demands for an undogmatic Christianity served a useful purpose and helped to counterbalance the tendency of theologians to regard the faith from too intellectual a point of view, to the negelct of its application to life itself. Pusey had written to Stanley in 1864

[1] *Letters*, p. 141.

on this matter: 'I think that one of the great dangers of the present day is to conceive of matters of faith as if they were matters of opinion.'[1] This attitude, it need hardly be said, did not apply to all, or even the majority of, theologians, and Westcott had nobly protested against any such conception. In the very year after Pusey's letter to Stanley he had written in the preface to *The Gospel of the Resurrection*: 'The subject *is not a vain thing for us: it is our life.*'

But if the reaction from too intellectual a presentation of Christianity had its healthy side, it was undoubtedly exaggerated, and led to an underrating of all dogma. This was perhaps strange in an age which was not averse to dogmatism in other spheres, some scientists were exceedingly dogmatic, and it seemed as though the theologian alone was to be deprived of the privilege. Those who thus disparaged Christian dogma ignored the indisputable fact that creed and conduct are closely allied, and that the one is largely dependent upon the other. On this, as on so many other matters, Lightfoot has contributed the last word: 'Christianity, it is said, is a life, not a creed. It could more truly be called "a life in a creed."'[2] The nineteenth century was unduly optimistic when it thought that the Christian way of life and Christian ethical standards could be preserved in isolation. We ourselves have learned in much bitterness that the fruits of Christianity cannot long survive where the roots of Christian dogmatic beliefs are lacking.

The refusal to accept dogma was bound sooner or later to rob the Faith of its effectiveness. When *Ecce Homo* was published in 1866 Westcott commented: 'It is this so-called Christian morality as the "sum of the Gospel" which makes Christianity so powerless now.'[3]

[1] *Life of Stanley*, II, p. 165.   [2] *Notes on Epistles of St. Paul*, p. 186.
[3] *Life*, I, p. 289.

That surely is true; for the attempt to reduce Christianity to a bare morality leaves man very much to his own resources and is in reality only another form of naturalism. Even to the question *Why* must I do right? it gives but an uncertain answer; and in face of the further question, *How* am I to do right? it is even more helpless. Moreover it views things too exclusively from a human standpoint and forgets that the Father desires the worship, as well as the obedience, of His children.

Such a reduced Christianity, even if men could be persuaded to accept it, has no real message of hope for those who are tied and bound by the weight of their sins and bewildered by the darkness which surrounds them. It is certainly far removed from the historic faith which found expression in the lives of the saints, and inspired countless thousands to witness to it by their deaths. May I close by quoting to you the moving words with which Neville Figgis ended the second of his Hulsean Lectures, words which I had the great privilege of hearing when they were first uttered: 'Take from the Christian faith its mystery and strangeness, and see what is left. Is the creed when "trimmed and stripped of all that touches the skies" a beautiful or even a helpful thing? . . . Leave out, if you must, the mysterious birth, the availing death, the empty tomb, and the sacramental presence, and what would you have left? Would it be very much to live by? Would it be anything at all to die for?'[1]

[1] *The Gospel and Human Needs*, p. 55.

Lecture Six

THE POSITION AT THE CLOSE OF THE CENTURY

WHEN allowance has been made for a number of developments which we have already considered it may be said that the position at the close of the century had not greatly changed from what it was in 1860. Many of the same problems were still pressing for solution, though the lapse of two generations had altered their form, and now they were becoming more urgent, because more widely known and realized owing to the spread of education and the publicity which had come from controversy. In addition many new facts and ideas had to be dealt with. If a renewed study of Greek theology and a better understanding with science had eased the situation in some respects, it cannot be said that theologians had adequately met the demands made upon them. But this was not so obvious then as it is to us. Many people imagined that all necessary adjustments had been made, and that nothing more need be feared from the advance of knowledge. The orthodox were certainly very optimistic, and a writer in *The Quarterly Review*, commenting on *Robert Elsmere* in 1888, actually spoke of the critical process as 'a phase of thought long ago lived through and practically dead.' Even Bishop Creighton seems to have shared this view, for as late as 1896 he could write, 'For my part I believe that the attack on Christianity is intellectually repulsed.'[1]

[1] *Life*, II, p. 191.

I

One factor which made for optimism was the realization that the older rationalism had proved unsatisfactory. This was admitted by Herbert Spencer when he wrote: 'Religious creeds, which in one way or another occupy the sphere that material interpretation seeks to occupy and fails the more it seeks, I have come to regard with a sympathy based on community of need.'[1] Science itself was moving away from a purely mechanistic idea of the universe and its conflict with religion was waning. On the other hand the full implication of scientific discoveries had not yet been realized.

For many believers the coming of a new century brought the hope of an era of affirmation and faith far different from the spirit of doubt and hesitancy which had marked the Victorian age. Men felt that they had gone through Purgatory, and could now rest awhile in the Earthly Paradise they had won, little realizing that ahead of them lay no Paradise, but the Inferno of two world wars. But even if there had been no wars it is doubtful if such an attitude could have been maintained. Humanity constantly endeavours to make for itself a quiet garden cut off from the surrounding chaos; but inevitably its peace is broken by that latent spirit of curiosity which cannot remain asleep, 'the Serpent, that never allows man to abide long in any Eden.'[2]

Yes, the lull could not last, for its origin lay in ignorance and the shutting out of unpleasant facts. Much was to come to disturb it; from a more drastic biblical criticism, from the study of comparative religion, and perhaps above all from the new psychology.

As regards biblical criticism it had come to be recognized that the Old Testament was not after all so important as people had supposed, and liberal views were

---

[1] *Autobiography*, II, p. 471.
[2] Berenson, *The Italian Painters of the Renaissance*, p. 174.

no longer regarded as highly dangerous. In 1894 Huxley wrote: 'Thirty years ago, criticism of "Moses" was held by most respectable people to be a deadly sin; now it has sunk to the rank of a mere peccadillo.'[1] As to the New Testament there was a comfortable feeling that the Cambridge school had broken the attack upon it. 'What Bishop Lightfoot has tested and approved, we believe we may accept as proven,' wrote J. B. Mayor in 1897, though he was careful to add, 'so far as present lights go.'[2] It was not then anticipated that principles which had been accepted for the Old Testament would be applied as ruthlessly to the New; whilst the storm which would rage round eschatology had hardly broken. Eschatology would, indeed, bring much distress of mind to simple souls, for the figure of Jesus thus presented, so far as it was intelligible, seemed repellent rather than attractive.

The deeper implications of comparative religion were also hidden. It was, indeed, recognized that Christianity had no monopoly of spiritual teaching and achievement; but other faiths, apart from Judaism and Islam, because they had little concern for morals, seemed to rank as philosophical systems rather than religions. The threat to the faith contained in attempts to account for both Judaism and Christianity as purely natural developments such as the rest, was scarcely understood except by scholars.

The most dangerous threat, however, was to come from psychology, for it offered an explanation of that religious intuition which for many, and especially for Evangelicals, was the surest evidence of the truth of their faith. This new challenge to orthodox Christianity found definite, if moderate, expression in William James's

[1] *Science and the Christian Tradition*, p. xi.
[2] *The Epistle of St. James*, p. cxlix.

Gifford Lectures (1901–2) on *The Varieties of Religious Experience*. James himself was a Christian of an undogmatic kind, which made his work more alarming, for earlier attempts to account for religious experiences by the application of psychology had come from open enemies, such as Bain's *The Senses and the Intellect* (1855) and Herbert Spencer's *Principles of Psychology* (1870–2).

The study of psychology was no new thing, it goes back at least as far as Aristotle's *De Anima*, and there is perhaps no more searching treatment of the subject than *The Confessions* of St. Augustine; but now it was making more ambitious claims for itself, in spite of the cold-shouldering of scientists. A new era in the study may be dated from the opening of the psychological laboratory at Leipzig by Wundt in 1875. Whatever view might be taken of psychology, and of its claim to be a science, no one could deny the increasing awareness of the mutual effects of mind upon mind, and of mind upon matter. Hort was willing to grant that no mental or spiritual movement took place without a 'concomitant physical movement.'[1]

Before our period the importance of psychology for religion had been realized by Schleiermacher, and in 1878 Bishop Boyd Carpenter expounded its uses in his Hulsean Lectures *The Witness of the Heart to Christ*. Earlier still, Jowett, anticipating the alarm which might follow its application, had written: 'Why should it be thought incredible that God should give law and order to the spiritual no less than to the natural creation?'[2]

But to admit that spiritual experiences might be conditioned by mental or bodily states and even to recognize that these might follow definite laws was one thing; to dismiss them as dependent on such states

[1] *The Way, the Truth, the Life*, p. 188.
[2] *The Epistles of St. Paul*, II, p. 235.

something very different. Some extreme advocates of the new psychology even ranked all spiritual phenomena as pathological, an attitude of mind which William James denounced as 'Medical Materialism.'[1] None the less much consternation was caused by the attempt to discount religion as merely subjective, 'an uprush from the subconscious self,' with the desire for salvation as an expression of the instinct for self-preservation, and prayer nothing more than a form of auto-suggestion. These notions were often accompanied by the patronizing admission that religion might be a useful thing, even if its truth was a matter of indifference.

The fact was that some psychologists were apparently unaware that they were dealing with means, and not with ends, and that their material was supplied solely by human consciousness. To explain the origin and development of a process is not to account for it, nor to assess its real significance. In the case of prayer, for example, to say that it is mere self-suggestion leaves unexplained the self which makes the suggestions.

Meanwhile liberal views were spreading in all directions and were even finding their way into books of reference such as the *Encyclopaedia Britannica*.[2] Many, however, seem to have been blind to their progress, and in 1884 it was stated that 'the Broad Church party had been extinguished by popular clamour.' This drew a rejoinder from a young Oxford don, Hastings Rashdall by name, who replied in *The Oxford Magazine* that on the contrary it had succeeded in 'leavening the tone of theological thought and theological temper among the clergy and religious world at large.'[3]

Perhaps the most striking illustration of the way in which liberal views had spread was the reception of *Lux*

---

[1] *The Varieties of Religious Experience*, p. 13.
[2] See above, p. 70.   [3] *Life*, p. 45.

Mundi. It caused, as we have seen, some commotion among the older Anglo-Catholics, but nothing to be compared with that aroused by earlier writings of a liberal trend. The veteran Archdeacon Denison, who in his younger days had taken a strong line against *Essays and Reviews*, admitted that he would no longer be willing to sign the denunciation of that work.[1] Another token was the pacific acceptance of R. L. Ottley's Bampton Lectures *On the Incarnation* in 1897; upon which Hastings Rashdall remarked, 'In 1860 the saintly Ottley would have been a persecuted heretic.'[2]

Thus liberal views were being imbibed unconsciously by many who would have indignantly refused the title of Broad Churchmen; but apart from the latter the open welcome of such views was exceptional. Evangelicals were still hampered by mutual suspicion and distrust, and not yet prepared to move forward. With the Anglo-Catholics things were better, for at Oxford the *Lux Mundi* group, in strong contrast with the pessimism of Liddon, were eager to disburden Christianity of dead values, and to demonstrate that the new knowledge could be used to the strengthening and purifying of the Catholic Faith. 'We did not desire to die in the last ditch,' wrote Scott Holland looking back in later years, 'but to throw defences and ramparts behind us, and to charge with flags flying, and see what we could do with a clear field and no favour.'[3]

This was a noble spirit and perhaps only possible for those who were in a position to understand and assess the value of the new ideas. Scholars had established their right to liberty of investigation, unhampered by obsolete conceptions of the authority of the Bible or the Church; but they were well aware that both Bible and Church

[1] Bell, *Randall Davidson*, p. 109.   [2] *Life*, p. 86.
[3] *A Bundle of Memories*, p. 58.

still possessed worth and authority, though it might be of a different kind.[1] For the people the situation was very different. They knew that both the Church and the Bible were being criticized and could no longer be accepted without question, and what authority was left to those who were incapable of thinking things out for themselves? As a consequence some sought refuge in the Church of Rome, which claimed to be infallible; others in Fundamentalism. But the great majority gradually lapsed into indifference. This is a frequent accompaniment of times of religious controversy. So it had been in the days of the Reformation, for 'the great mass of mankind take these things for granted and any event which leads them to think that the institutions of life are not as divinely fixed as the everlasting hills is sure to precipitate [the wildest disorder.]'[2] Even some extreme liberals became alarmed at the decay of religious belief among the common folk. Robert Lowe, famous for his saying that 'We must educate our masters,' wrote to Jowett: 'If religion (whether true or false?) goes what will you put in its place?'

Faced by the weakening of external authority many turned to the witness of the lives of Christians as the most powerful argument for the truth of Christianity.[3] This is, indeed, much more potent than any formal apologetic and carries a wider appeal, since it can be made to those who have no opportunity of studying theological questions at first hand.[4] Others sought proof from internal assurance and in what may be called mysticism,

---

[1] Cf. Streeter, *Restatement and Reunion*, p. 39. 'Authority must necessarily occupy a far more important place in religion than in any other department of thought or life.'

[2] Allen, *The Continuity of Christian Thought*, p. 296.

[3] This argument was elaborated by Francis Paget in *Studies in the Christian Character* (1895).

[4] Cf. Streeter's essay on 'The Simplicity of Christianity,' in *Restatement and Reunion*, pp. 1ff.

the direct experience by the believer of the God whom he worships. There was, of course, nothing novel in this; Coleridge, for example, had found help from the writings of the German mystics, whilst George Fox and William Law had been to him 'a pillar of fire by night in the wilderness of doubt' through which he had travelled before finding intellectual satisfaction in the system of Kant. But now it was being worked out in a more scientific and systematic manner. Martineau, in *The Seat of Authority in Religion* (1890), claimed that there was a faculty in man which enabled him to recognize the working of God in nature, in history, and in humanity. About the same time Inge, who had just migrated from Cambridge to Oxford, began to study Christian Mysticism in 'order to find a sound intellectual basis' for his religious beliefs.[1] One result of his studies was the Bampton Lectures of 1899 which aroused wide interest and placed mysticism on a new footing, redeeming it from the reproach of haziness and even unorthodoxy which had, for many thoughtful people, enveloped it. There was, indeed, a growing interest in the subject in literary circles, fostered by the Celtic school and by the writings of Theodore Watts-Dunton, whose essay on 'The Renascence of Wonder' in Chambers' *Cyclopaedia of English Literature* attracted much attention, as did his novel *Aylwin*, first published in 1898.

Mysticism and a reliance on spiritual intuition, however, though they might help those who were religious by nature or upbringing to bolster up their faith, were of little avail to common men and women for whom the traditional religion, received on authority, had had no verification in personal experience. Confused and disquieted many of them abandoned religion as a matter beyond their comprehension and drifted into indifference

[1] *Vale*, p. 32.

and agnosticism. Their confusion and uncertainty were aggravated by the freedom with which religious questions were discussed in the public press; often by those quite unqualified to deal with such matters. Fancy religions also arose to satisfy man's religious needs, and these too added to the prevailing confusion.

The age was over-critical and apt to concentrate on the defects of all systems of belief, especially if they were traditional. In the past people had believed what they wished to believe, now the process had gone into reverse, and negation was exalted into a merit. Men had struggled to attain religious freedom and the right to believe as they chose, and now found themselves robbed of all settled belief. One thing seemed as good as another and nothing had any abiding significance; all had become relative, but with no standard to which it could be related.

Even among regular church-goers there were many who were content to acquiesce in this state of uncertainty. Religion then, as so frequently, was mainly the property of the middle classes, and attendance at divine worship a sign rather of respectability than a confession of faith in Christ. As a consequence they did not trouble their minds or face their difficulties.

Englishmen are notoriously suspicious of speculation and dislike hard and prolonged thinking, and so they were unwilling, save for the few, to go deeply into the matter, and simply put religious questions aside as incapable of solution.[1] Some, in accord with the prevailing humanitarian spirit, did so deliberately, for any inquiry might only lead to futher perplexity and mental suffering. There can be no doubt that the most serious

[1] Cf. *Letters of J. A. Symonds*, p: 49. 'We are . . . now too interested in phenomena, too bent on actual discovery to embark on speculation. Yet this is one-sided . . . we are contented with the examination of matter and neglect the problems of the mind.'

enemy of religion was the cowardice or levity which prevented men from thinking things out.[1] Fred Bason, the Bermondsey bookseller, belongs to a later period, but his comment on the poor demand for theological literature can be applied to conditions at the end of the nineteenth century. 'Why,' he asks, 'don't religion sell? Do people know all about God?'[2]

The Church seemed strangely indifferent to the crisis through which it was passing. It is true that the press and the religious weeklies were full of accounts of what was called the Crisis in the Church—but these were concerned, not with the things which really mattered, but with squabbles over the Ornaments' rubric. This dispute had just robbed the Church of England of one of the wisest and greatest of her bishops, for there can be little doubt that attempts to deal with it had shortened the life of Bishop Creighton.

We have thus the beginnings of that spirit of indifference which has reached such terrible proportions in our own day, when sport and the cinema have almost completely displaced more serious matters in the mind of the average man and woman. People will not be bothered by such matters as their sins and shortcomings, and are averse to subjects which may disturb that state of mental torpor which is based on the refusal to face fundamentals.

Thus interest in religion was gradually decaying or turning to other things. How different it had been in the Middle Ages when, as in Chaucer's time, the lengthening days of spring and summer urged men on pilgrimage to Canterbury or other shrines; now they were wending their way to Brighton or Southend, to Blackpool or the

[1] Cf. Quick, *Doctrines of the Creed*, p. 6: 'The real faithlessness of the modern world is seen in its half-despairing, half-complacent agreement to give up ultimate questions.'

[2] *Fred Bason's Diary* (edited by Nicholas Bentley), p. 26.

Isle of Man. The not inconsiderable number who still professed interest in religion were not taken very seriously, it was merely their hobby. And, indeed, there was undoubtedly a risk that the Church might become 'a school of culture in the religious art for persons of leisure and education.'[1]

It would, of course, be idle to deny that there was still interest in religion. But its emphasis tended to shift away from religion in its organized forms, and to concentrate on its practical rather than its dogmatic aspects. Philanthropy, not doctrine, seemed all-important, and to strive to help others a sufficient expression of religious faith. Here your own city gained a certain fortuitous notoriety in a popular limerick:

> There was an old lady of Leeds
> Who tried, in turn, all the creeds.
>   When disgusted she found
>   That each left her aground,
> She attended to other folk's needs.

There were, too, many sincerely religious souls who, having been brought up in the atmosphere of the Church, felt themselves no longer able to use its ministrations and drifted away. Some form of Unitarianism might have satisfied them, but they were repelled by its ugliness and provincialism, and so ceased to maintain contact with religion, seeking to fill their lives with other expressions of the spirit, art and music, and allied forms of spiritual enterprise. Even Browning's influence was declining, and literary critics were condemning what they regarded as his rather morbid interest in religion, though still full of admiration for his less intellectual poems with their emotional insight and glowing splendour of colour.[2]

---

[1] J. H. Skrine, *Pastor Futurus*, p. 10.
[2] It must not, however, be forgotten that Henry Jones' *Browning as a Religious and Philosophical Teacher* appeared in 1891.

Yet all the time there was a wistful looking back and a feeling of unsatisfied longing. You can see it in Thomas Hardy's poem, *The Oxen*.

> I feel
> If someone said on Christmas Eve
> Come, let us see the oxen kneel
> . . . I should go with him in the gloom
> Hoping it might be so.

Of actual opposition to Christianity there was but little, and that not of much account. The real threat to the future of religion lay not in those who openly attacked it, but in those who passed it by as a thing indifferent. There were, of course, political extremists who regarded all religion as a definite enemy to be destroyed if possible, but they were but few. Many also regarded organized religion with suspicion as being part of a plan of the possessing classes to keep them quiet, or as a sign of respectability. The majority of those outside the Church felt that its teaching had no meaning for them and were entirely unconcerned about its message. Religion was no longer a vital question, it had become one of life's luxuries not one of its necessities.

A grave consequence of the loss of authority by religion and the Church was a progressive decline in morals. There were those who found in the uncertainty about the truths of Christianity a welcome excuse for throwing off its moral restraints, which they had resented, but not overtly denied. The last decade of the century saw a growth of 'levity, if not of laxity' which made the term 'the naughty nineties' no misnomer.[1] Those who in the earlier part of our period had attacked Christian dogmas had had a naïve belief that Christian morals would remain unaffected. They failed to realize the extent to which moral standards are dependent on fixed

[1] G. M. Trevelyan, *English Social History*, p. 568.

beliefs. Any merely pragmatic standard is most unreliable, for it is largely conditioned by the moral quality
of the contemporary society. But by the end of the
century Christian ethics themselves were beginning to be
called in question and the religious basis of morality
criticized in the name of scientific humanism.

A mechanical view of the universe not only challenged
the supernatural claims of Christianity, but also the
sanctions underlying its ethics. Religion was thus
robbed of all power to arouse any idea of obligation,
or even of responsibility, in the individual. At the same
time the extension of the theory of physical evolution
from the race to the individual weakened any sense of
sin. Sin, so called, might be due to nothing more than
the survival of animal instincts which would gradually
be eliminated or overcome.

The effects of the changed position in regard to
morality took some time to manifest themselves. For in
these matters, as Oman has said, 'Habit and custom often
confuse the issue. Men cannot rid themselves at once of
old associations, old views, old habits.'[1] But such
habits tended in any case to decay with the growing
complexity of life. When the relations of man and man
are concerned, as they are in small communities, with
persons known to each other, they have force; but when
they are transferred to vague and massive entities this
force is often lost. Hence, probably a growing dis-
respect for law.

One great difficulty of those who are anxious to
maintain or elevate ethical standards is that popular
morality is so largely sentimental and emotional, and so
little controlled by principles. 'Generosity ranks far
before justice, sympathy before truth, love before
chastity, a pliant and obliging disposition before a

[1] *Vision and Authority*, pp. 180f.

rigidly honest one. In brief, the less admixture of intellect required for the practice of any virtue, the higher it stands in popular estimation.'[1]

As late as 1908 Dr. Figgis could claim that a new spirit was at work, counteracting the doubts and hesitations of the Victorian age. But that was true only of a few of the finer spirits, such as J. M. Keynes and his friends, who set forth 'the assertion of truth, the unveiling of illusion, the dissipation of hate, the enlargement of men's minds and hearts,' as their ideals. Under the surface, however, and in the popular mind, there was a general decay of ideals, and, in spite of outward peace and self-complacency, the seeds of the coming tragic years were slowly maturing.

An impassioned opponent of natural selection had once exclaimed, 'Leave me my ancestors in Paradise, and I will grant you yours in the Zoological Gardens.' But the real danger was not ancestors in the Zoo, but the growth of the feeling that man was merely a superior kind of animal, bereft of any spiritual endowments. If such a view of humanity is once accepted all man's endeavours will be confined to providing himself with what are in effect nothing more than the most convenient and hygienic cages. There lay the danger. Man was concentrating his thoughts on the things of this life, and forgetting his eternal destiny; the growth of comfort and security had weakened his spiritual and moral sinews. This complacent and lethargic spirit had even invaded the religious world, and many of those who still outwardly accepted the Christian belief demanded a cheap and easy faith. In the words of the ancient Ionian proverb, they were content 'to worship God with other people's incense.'[2]

---

[1] C. F. G. Masterman, *The Condition of England*, p. 115.
[2] Cf. Pausanias, IX, xxx. 1.

In spite of doubts and hesitation over ultimate things the men of the Victorian era had been very confident about worldly issues. Their achievements in material things had been such as no previous age could rival, and this gave them an unshakeable optimism. Civilization was not yet at the cross-roads, and any notion that its survival might be threatened was very far from their thoughts. But by the end of our period this boundless confidence was beginning to wear a little thin, as though the weariness of a dying century had come upon them. The sudden outbreak of the South African war with its early reverses had made some to pause. War had seemed so remote a thing, and now its head had been raised amidst the comforts and securities of the present. This gave occasion for Bishop Gore to preach on the last day of the century what his biographer calls 'a most des- pondent sermon on the hollowness of modern progress.'[1]

But the bishop was right, for the popular belief in inevitable progress was a mere superstition, without any justification in either history or science. Science itself, in the person of Huxley, dealt the whole conception a shrewd blow, for in his Romanes Lecture for 1893 he affirmed that nothing in science gave it any assured support.

The material prosperity upon which so many vaunted themselves, like Tyre of old, was based on a system which contained many flaws, and these might at any time bring about its collapse; those social injustices which a some- what tardy legislation had done little to mitigate, the spirit of competition, and the scramble for international markets. Looking back we can clearly discern the gulf between the facts as they actually were and the way in which men, apart from a few thinkers and social re- formers, insisted on regarding them.

In theology and in religion also there were similar

[1] *Life*, p. 225.

gaps. In fact theology and religion had moved apart.
There was little understanding of the work of theologians
among the working clergy and ministers, and they
themselves often held views which they dared not
proclaim in their naked truth to their congregations.
Most of them were too much immersed in practical
affairs to make time for reading after they had left the
university or theological college, and contented themselves with the occasional perusal of small handbooks or
the guidance of their favourite religious journal. Even
had they desired to continue study the necessary books
were beyond their means, and, in addition, they often
lacked guidance, though help was forthcoming for some
from Clerical Reading Societies, whilst the foundation
of the Central Society for Sacred Study in 1899 did real
service.

Those who, in spite of all difficulties, succeeded in
keeping up their reading, often felt that scholars did not
deal with the real problems which confronted them in
their ministerial life. The language used was often almost
unintelligible and the whole outlook of theologians
seemed to have little relation to the life of the present.
Men of scholarly mind, as they brood beside 'their
studious lamps,' are apt to regard theology as a kind of
abstract science which raises interesting problems for the
intellect, and to forget that for the majority uncertainty
in matters of religion may be a grievous hardship. For
them at least there is urgent need of

> some sure
> Song in the dark, some story against fear.

But religion must be based on truth, and the truths which
were being enunciated by scholars, unrelated though
they might seem to be to practical life, could only be
ignored to the ultimate hurt of religion itself;

little profit brings
Speed in the van and blindness in the rear.

If the gap between theology and religion was harmful to
faith, since without intellectual examination it may so
easily degenerate into superstition, it also had drawbacks
for theologians, for 'theology, however much it may be
a matter of revelation in the sources of its knowledge,
must be a science of experience in putting its truth to the
test.'[1] Moreover the circumstance that most theologians
live in universities tends to make them regard themselves
rather as members of an academic society than as teachers
responsible to a Church.

But if there was a gulf between the study and the
pulpit there was an equally dangerous gap between the
pulpit and the pew.[2] This arose from two not unrelated
causes. ·Preachers who could no longer accept certain
traditional doctrines preferred to concentrate on practical
teaching and on such matters as they still held in common
with their people. Others exercised a deliberate reserve,
not wishing to upset the faith of simple people who were
in no position to understand the difficulties raised by
science and biblical criticism.

Such an economy in dealing with truth may, however,
have unfortunate consequences, fostering the idea among
the more educated that the clergy preach things which
they do not themselves believe. Congregations often
have a much greater awareness of difficulties than their
ministers suppose, owing to newspaper reports and even
to their own reading, and if preachers ignore such
difficulties, the suggestion is that they are unable to meet
them. In 1890 Archbishop Benson was amazed to
discover that a group of highly educated churchwomen

---

[1] Oman, *Vision and Authority*, p. 190.
[2] See some interesting comments on this subject in Hamilton, *The People of
God*, I, pp. xx, ff.

K

whom he was instructing were dubious as to the authorship of St. John, very uncertain as to whether we really
know anything of the life of our Lord, and unwilling
to accept the personality of the Holy Ghost.[1] So, too,
C. F. G. Masterman, writing a little later than 1900, has
said that 'definite statements of the average belief, set out
in black and white by the average congregation, would
astonish the average preacher.'[2]

The matter is certainly beset with difficulties. No man,
of course, ought to teach doctrines in which he no longer
believes, but on the other hand, as the representative of a
Church, he may have to teach matters about which he is
uncertain.[3] In his desire not to offend the older people,
however, he must not inculcate the young with views
which will inevitably have to be abandoned and be the
cause of unnecessary doubt and unsettlement.

Such considerations, however, do not affect the
theologian who is bound to proclaim what he believes to
be true, even if it involves doubt and unsettlement for
individual believers. Creighton, in his younger days,
held that 'unintelligent acquiescence in opinions, though
these might be true, was immoral and dangerous.'[4]

At the end of the century there was still much obscurantism, due in part to the cowardice which seeks refuge
in conventions and the mental stagnation which is
content with formulas. But much of it was also due to
the unwillingness to abandon teaching which had proved
so effective in the past, and was still found effective in the
present. This was, of course, especially true of the
Evangelicals and their scheme of salvation. After all,

---

[1] *Life*, II, p. 299.   [2] *The Condition of England*, p. 18.
[3] Morley in *Compromise* attacked the intellectual honesty of men who
when ordained at twenty-three, committed themselves more or less blindly
to the acceptance of certain positions, not knowing what the future may bring
in the way of new knowledge and experience.
[4] *Life*, I, p. 36, and cf. above, p. 90.

what the ordinary man so sorely needed was not up-to-date knowledge, but forgiveness and power. Hence Canon Ainger's protest:

> With eager knife that oft has sliced
> At Gentile gloss or Jewish fable,
> Before the crowd you lay the Christ
>   Upon the Lecture table.
>
> From bondage to the old beliefs
> You say our rescue must begin—
> But *I*—want refuge from my griefs,
>   And saving from my sin.[1]

But obscurantism was not confined to orthodox Christians. In Lord Keynes' memoirs, to which I have already referred, we have a description of an intellectual atmosphere in which the non-existence of God and the falsity of Christianity were so much taken for granted that any attempt to discuss them would have been regarded as ridiculous.

This summary dismissal of Christianity was due in large measure to the idea that believers still clung obstinately to myths, legends, and traditions which had been discredited by modern advances in knowledge, and, as a matter of fact, had been abandoned by thinking believers. Even to-day people outside the Church still imagine that it accepts verbal inspiration, hell fire, and a material heaven 'with streets of shining gold,' as well as the miracles of the Old Testament.

To meet the objections of those who still misunderstood Christianity and to wean the ultra-orthodox from their untenable position there was urgent need for re-statement. For as Hort said, 'In order to preserve and restore, it was necessary to advance.'[2]   Apologetics

---

[1] 'On reading a Volume of Modern Sermons.'
[2] *The Way, the Truth, the Life*, p. 24.

K*

certainly took on a new tone, for instead of being content
to deal with objections to the faith, they adopted a more
positive method and tried to demonstrate the worth of
Christianity as an explanation of the scheme of things.
In so doing they tried to combine the traditional teaching
of the Church with what had become known through
advances in secular knowledge. This was the only
effective policy, for any vital religion must be perpetually
renewed and reinvigorated by the new truths which God
Himself is ever disclosing.

It has, however, to be admitted that theology did not
rise fully to meet the new situation, though much was
being undertaken. Dr. Lock ended his inaugural lecture
in 1896 with these words: 'There is at the present
moment no sphere of study, unless it be that of natural
science, in which there is so much of movement, of
progress, of fresh light, and so certain assurance that toil
will meet with its due reward.'[1] But though many new
books were produced the efforts of theologians were
largely uncoordinated and dispersed. Much theological
writing was of the nature of mere palliatives, intended to
meet present needs, and any long-term or comprehensive
policy was lacking. The nearest approach to it was in
Lux Mundi, and that was only possible through the
presence in and near Oxford of a number of remarkable
men. Compared with the growing richness of religious
experience theology was comparatively barren. In other
words the intellectual presentation of the Christian faith
was not keeping pace with its practical and emotional
expressions. Theology 'is the history of the Church's
soul. The work of the theologian . . . is to keep the
record up to date.'[2] Some of this failure was due to the
gulf between religion and theology to which reference

[1] *The Bible and Christian Life*, p. 96.
[2] J. H. Skrine, *Pastor Futurus*, p. 141.

has already been made, for unless the theologian himself
has a living faith and experience his writings will be
stale and unprofitable.

But to 'keep the record up to date' is no easy matter,
for theology must be cautious, even hesitating; whilst a
religion which is truly living is ever stretching out
towards fresh goals. Theologians were undoubtedly
timid. Perhaps they feared the condemnation of
ecclesiastical authorities or popular outcry if they were
too venturesome. But I think that the chief cause was
the realization that too much still remained uncertain
and also that they had inadequate knowledge, in that age
of specialization, of other studies. Theology was no
longer the queen of the sciences for her subjects had
become unruly.

There was one man who might have undertaken the
task of restatement with some prospect of success, and
that was Hort. But he was strangely tongue-tied, in
spite of many appeals, and his only major contribution,
the Hulsean Lectures of 1871, was not published until
after his death. He had made many additions and
alterations, without reaching any final satisfaction. Even
so, *The Way, the Truth, the Life* was one of the most
valuable works in English theology during our period.
Its chief value lay, not in any attempt to provide facile
answers to current criticism, but in the putting forth of a
point of view or method by which truth as a whole was
to be approached. This method had brought conviction
to one earnest inquirer, though he regarded himself as
still a learner, and was content that his work should
suggest more questions than it answered.

The end of the period and the years which immediately
followed it was marked by a decline of interest in pure
theology. In Biblical studies there was too great a
concentration on the text of documents and their

linguistic and historical aspects, a necessary stage no doubt if firm foundations were to be laid, but it robbed theology of its vitality. In acknowledging the gift of Moule's inaugural lecture as Norrisian Professor at Cambridge in 1899, Gwatkin wrote: 'I think that our Cambridge school is getting too much absorbed in prolegomena and literary details and needs a call to higher and wider things.'[1] In the same year Pringle-Pattison, a sympathetic observer, had written to Hastings Rashdall: 'The surprising thing is that in the great Church of England there is so little of the leaven of thinking Christianity. And it has so good an historical title to exist in the Anglican Church with its Cambridge School of Christian Platonists.'[2]

The truth of the matter was that not many of the clergy of the Church of England were interested in theology. The period had seen much admirable activity in the parishes and a great extension of social work and of missionary effort, and in these the energies of some very able men had been absorbed. Among the Anglo-Catholics many ardent souls were much more anxious about the ritual rather than the intellectual expression of the faith, and, indeed, the extent to which ritual disputes had obscured the danger of attacks on the faith from without aroused the amazed wonder of Randall Davidson, the future archbishop.[3]

Another circumstance that militated against any comprehensive restatement of the faith was that theology was out of touch with philosophy. But this was no very serious deprivation since philosophy itself was in a state of confusion. In France there had been a strong reaction from the dogmatic assumptions of Positivism, and at the

[1] Harford and Macdonald, *Bishop Handley Moule*, p. 153.
[2] Matheson, *The Life of Hastings Rashdall*, pp. 92f.
[3] Bell, *Randall Davidson*, p. 153.

close of the nineteenth century philosophy everywhere was striving to liberate itself from this tyranny. Moreover philosophy had also failed to assimilate the new knowledge and its division into antagonistic schools had lowered its prestige. For philosophers, in the words of Professor Caldecott, the century was 'closing in a mood of depression through our failure to secure a commanding and dominant result . . . after so much mental activity.'[1]

For theology, too, the century was closing with its tasks unfulfilled, though the extent of the failure of the liberal experiment was not realized. But if its accomplishments had been mainly negative they had not been useless, for reconstruction ever involves some destruction of the old. And there were a few enlightened souls who saw this clearly:

> I looked and lo ! 'mid the decay,
>   The Waster was the Builder too;
> And when the dust-cloud rolled away,
>   I saw the new.

The uncertainty might be distressing and seem entirely harmful, but as Keats has reminded us in his poem on 'Autumn,' 'a season of mists' may also be one of 'mellow fruitfulness.' There was need for patience and suspension of judgment. The flood of new knowledge must neither be dammed up nor allowed free course. If men were compelled to give up beliefs which had seemed to be an integral part of the faith, that had happened before, and later ages, as they looked back, had seen in the process the good hand of God leading them to truer knowledge of Himself.

So the task which they left unfulfilled remains as a challenge; and it is our burden and our privilege to undertake it. The years which have elapsed since the end

[1] *The Philosophy of Religion*, p. v.

of the nineteenth century are actually more numerous
than those covered by this course and in them things have
moved fast and far.   The influx of knowledge has
continued at an even greater pace, whilst the moral
influence of religion has decayed.   Intellectual uncertainty
has led many to seek a refuge in crude dogmatisms of
various hues, just as the similar phenomenon in the
political world has made totalitarianism the haven of
those who despair of freedom.   One crying need of our
day is for prophets to guide us,

> The kings of thought
> Who wage contention with their time's decay.

But our age is unwilling to listen to prophets, even if we
had them, and their voices would be drowned in the
hurry and clamour of the modern world.   And so the
task is laid on lesser people, men and women like ourselves.   If our contribution can be but small, it must not
be withheld; and even if it is the contribution of Christian
living rather than Christian thought, it may not be the
less valuable on that account, for ultimately our problems
will, I believe, be solved as much by saints as by savants.[1]
But the future as it lies before us is veiled and hazardous.

Dean Stanley as he faced the perplexities of his day
found consolation in the great figure in the book of
Isaiah: 'Who is this that cometh from Edom, that is
glorious in his apparel, travelling in the greatness of his
strength, leading his people through the deep as a horse
through the wilderness, that they should not stumble'
(lxiii. 1, 13).   May we not turn to another and more
hallowed figure?   For are we not like the disciples who
followed Jesus, wondering and afraid, on that last
decisive journey to Jerusalem?   Yet we have privileges

[1] Cf. Storr, *Development of English Theology*, etc., p. 157 'The task . . . which
confronts theology at the present time is the vindication of the spiritual.'

which they could not possess, for nearly two thousand years of Christian history have revealed to us many things about our Master which were hidden from their eyes. Above all we know, as they did not then know, that if the journey leads to the Cross, the Cross was but the prelude to the Resurrection, that out of apparent disaster final victory will surely come.